PRAISE FOR ASS

"*Assata Taught Me* is a maste. _____ ____ ___.__ ____ _____ Tradition. From the extractive structures of the world's largest police state to the revolutionary resistance, Donna Murch meticulously traces the history and contours of the current Movement for Black Lives. This book is seminal like its namesake, Assata Shakur."

—IBRAM X. KENDI, author of *How to Be an Antiracist*

"Donna Murch is one of the sharpest, most incisive, and elegant writers on racism, radicalism, and struggle today. In this collection of essays assessing the current contours of the contemporary movement against racism in the United States, Murch combines a historian's rigor with a cultural critic's insights and the passionate expression of someone deeply engaged with the politics, debates, and key questions confronting activists and organizers today. This is a smart and sophisticated book that should be read and studied by everyone in search of answers to the profound crises that continue to confront this country."

—KEEANGA-YAMAHTTA TAYLOR, author of
From #BlackLivesMatter to Black Liberation

"Donna Murch is one of our most brilliant thinkers and a committed scholar activist. In *Assata Taught Me,* she offers powerful insights about the Black freedom movement and Black radical politics, past and present. I always learn and am inspired when I read her work. This book is essential reading for historians, organizers, and people interested in making sense of this historical moment, and more importantly, in changing the world."

—BARBARA RANSBY, author of *Ella Baker
and the Black Freedom Movement*

"To feel anything other than fatalistic about the moment in which we currently live, and to see the future as anything less than perilous, might seem utterly foolish—unless, that is, one has sat with Donna

Murch's latest. With her rigorous rescuing, remembering, and reckoning with past histories of trauma, struggle, and resistance that current pundits and progressives alike too easily forget, as well as her searing reminders of present-day possibilities for a better world, Murch, like Assata Shakur before her, teaches us much we desperately need to learn in this time of momentous upheaval."

—HEATHER ANN THOMPSON, Pulitzer Prize–winning author of *Blood in the Water: The Attica Prison Uprising of 1971 of 1971 and its Legacy*

"Assata Shakur was a prisoner of war. Donna Murch understands this profoundly, which is why she wrote a book about a half-century of overlapping domestic wars in the United States. Each essay forcefully drives home the point that to be Black in America—to be Black in the world—is to live in a state of war under a warfare state. She writes history with fire, burning through decades of liberal obfuscation to reveal a world, not of 'activists' and 'interest groups,' but of combatants, collateral damage, refugees, and POWs. Assata has taught all of us, and her key lessons are found in these pages."

—ROBIN D.G. KELLEY, author of *Freedom Dreams: The Black Radical Imagination*

"In this essential collection of essays, Donna Murch sheds new light on the relationship between the Movement for Black Lives and the earlier practices and ideals of Black Power. She shows how the emergence of the largest police state, with its spectacular and mundane violence in the intervening years, has shaped the demands, organizations, and futures etched under the banner of Black Lives Matter. Written with verve and clarity, this is a book for our times."

—ADOM GETACHEW, author of *Worldmaking after Empire: The Rise and Fall of Self-Determination*

"Donna Murch is one of the most astute, fearless, and brilliant US historians working today. These essays are necessary to understand who we are now and how we got here."

—JASON STANLEY, author of *How Fascism Works*

ASSATA TAUGHT ME

State Violence, Racial Capitalism, and the Movement for Black Lives

DONNA MURCH

Haymarket Books
Chicago, Illinois

Published in 2022 by
Haymarket Books
P.O. Box 180165
Chicago, IL 60618
773-583-7884
www.haymarketbooks.org
info@haymarketbooks.org

ISBN: 978-1-64259-516-1

Distributed to the trade in the US through Consortium Book Sales and Distribution (www.cbsd.com) and internationally through Ingram Publisher Services International (www.ingramcontent.com).

This book was published with the generous support of Lannan Foundation and Wallace Action Fund.

Special discounts are available for bulk purchases by organizations and institutions. Please email info@haymarketbooks.org for more information.

Cover image of a mural depicting Assata Shakur in the ExhibitBe public art takeover of DeGaulle Manor housing complex in New Orleans, photographed by Irene Rible. Cover design by Rachel Cohen.

Printed in Canada by union labor.

Library of Congress Cataloging-in-Publication data is available.

10 9 8 7 6 5 4 3 2 1

For Carla Jean, Lucy Jean, and Madison Savannah

I believe in living.

I believe in birth.

I believe in the sweat of love

and in the fire of truth.

And i believe that a lost ship,

steered by tired, seasick sailors,

can still be guided home

to port.

Assata Shakur, "Affirmation"

CONTENTS

INTRODUCTION

Assata Taught Me, the title of this collection of essays, has a double meaning. The first references contemporary herstory of mobilization against racial violence; the second speaks to my own trajectory as a Black Panther historian. Since 2012, a new generation of activists has anointed the phrase through T-shirts, hoodies, protest banners, and murals as an expression not only of the militant spirit of the contemporary Black Lives Matter Movement (BLMM) but also of its continuities with the Black Radical organizing of generations past. In the early twenty-first century, an overwhelmingly Black, female-led social movement against state violence directed at African Americans throughout the United States has embraced Assata Shakur, a former rank-and-file member of the New York Black Panther Party (BPP) and Black Liberation Army (BLA), as a living embodiment of struggle.

The second meaning references my own politicization and introduction to the Black Panther Party through Shakur's writings in the twilight years of the Cold War. In 1987, Assata Shakur published her autobiography as a fugitive in Cuba, under the protection of Fidel Castro, with a phalanx of federal, state, and local US law enforcement in pursuit of her after a successful escape from the Clinton Correctional Facility for Women in New Jersey eight years before. The FBI placed a million-dollar bounty for her "capture dead or alive," a figure which the state of New Jersey later doubled. The timing of the publication of *Assata: An Autobiography* was incredibly significant, coming as it did during Ronald Reagan's second term in office, just on the cusp of the Iran–Contra hearings. Republicans had appropriated Martin Luther

1

King Jr.'s 1963 "I Have a Dream" speech while launching a sweeping assault on the victories of the Civil Rights Movement, including affirmative action, voting rights protections, and the expansion of the social welfare state. Black conservative Shelby Steele captured the spirit of this new color-blind racism with his anti-affirmative action screed *The Content of Our Character: A New Vision of Race in America*. Conservative pundits appropriated King's words to endorse a rollback of the hard-won victories of the postwar Black freedom struggle.[1]

In contrast to the uses and abuses of the Civil Rights Movement by its antagonists, Assata Shakur represented a counterhistory for my younger self. Starting in 1973, when Black communities throughout the United States created sanctuary spaces announcing "Assata Is Welcome Here," the fugitive revolutionary became a recurrent inspiration and icon for Black struggle internationally. In the late 1980s, Assata embodied a repressed history of resistance, Black Power, and Black Radicalism for a younger generation coming of age at the height of the Reagan era and its intensified domestic wars on drugs and crime that functioned as a de facto war on Black youth. Shakur's participation in the armed wing of the Black Liberation struggle, through a succession of trials, torture, and incarceration, made her the antithesis of a politics of conciliation and incorporation. For me, and others who followed, *Assata* opened a lens to a recent history of self-defense, Black internationalism, and left Pan-Africanism that defied the strictures of a narrowly defined domestic push for African American inclusion and upward mobility.[2]

As the final essay in this book shows, Assata's image and voice have become synonymous, once again, with Black youth mobilization against state violence. This was nowhere more evident to me than in a 2017 trip to Brazil, where I gave a talk at the Universidade Federal do Rio de Janeiro on the meaning of Assata Shakur and Black Marxism on the one hundredth anniversary of the Russian Revolution. Members of an independent organizing group called Occupy

Alemão in the north of Rio, which represented one of the largest complexes of informal communities known as favelas, invited me into the hearth and home of longtime organizer Zilda Chaves to talk about Assata. Favelas house an enormous portion of Rio's Black residents; estimates number between seven hundred and one thousand segmented areas throughout Brazil's second-largest metropolitan area. The communities are trellised into the sides of hills, mountains, and other difficult-to-access terrain that rarely have adequate public transportation. When I asked one of the members of Occupy Alemão about the difficulties of transportation, he looked at me with deep meaning in his eyes and explained, "When you are Black in Brazil, you learn to climb." With their roots stretching back to the post-emancipation era, favelas are urgent reminders for many Black Brazilians of slavery's continuities past and present.

As we struggled to communicate through translation, the young members of the group described Assata as an "embodiment of freedom" and a profound symbol of how the state attacks Black women through a combination of organized violence and social neglect. Assata's life dramatized the struggles of those closest to them: mothers, aunts, and grandmothers who continually face the consequences of state violence in its manifold forms, be they the hot violence of police killings or the cold violence of denying water, electricity, and the protection of state regulation to informal communities. The depth of their knowledge about Assata and the Black Panther Party more generally struck me, as did their interrogation of whether she should be understood through the lens of Pan-Africanism or Marxism, which they saw as antagonistic traditions. In their eyes, Assata Shakur embodied an alternate vision of Black womanhood that exemplified strength and resilience. Her commitment to armed struggle, successful escape from a maximum-security prison, and flight to Cuba spoke directly to the power of marronage and Quilombista organizing in Black, working-class Brazil.[3] Whether for those in northern Rio de Janeiro, or for me as a young college student in western Massachusetts in the late 1980s, or for the wide spectrum of groups who make up the contemporary Movement for Black Lives (M4BL), Assata is not only a powerful representational figure in the Black Radical imagination but also a catalyst for political education and mobilization throughout the globe.

The rich promise of possibility animates the essays in this volume, the core of which I wrote between 2014 and 2016 while living in the Crenshaw district, where I was researching a book on the effects of the drug war and crack crisis on Black Los Angeles. My research raised a number of difficult questions about the obstacles to mobilizing an organized response to state violence and mass incarceration in the years immediately following the Civil Rights and Black Power movements. The twilight years of the Cold War nurtured a bipartisan consensus on expanding the domestic wars on drugs and crime that proved so detrimental to a whole generation of older Black activists, including much-loved Black Panther Party members Michael Zinzun and Dedon Kamathi.[4] As I worked to piece together the local history of Black community response to the late twentieth-century wars on drugs and gangs in Los Angeles, one of its most important and iconic staging grounds, the Ferguson protests erupted on August 9, 2014. The explosion of protest in St. Louis's North County transformed the national dialogue on race and state violence by forcing the Department of Justice to reckon with an entrenched system of racial violence and resource extraction that enabled the killing of eighteen-year-old Michael Brown. While the stirrings of this movement stretched much further back in time and throughout the country, the Ferguson rebellion demonstrated that a larger historical arc connected the nation's intensified fifty-plus-year "war on crime" with the millennial articulation of a Movement for Black Lives.

One of the most fraught challenges of writing contemporary history is the somewhat arbitrary designation of when the story ends. The past and present are locked in a political dialectic in which the urgency of the moment always informs our chronicling of past events. In my case, this process was inverted, as my studies of Black Radicalism in the 1960s and 1970s inspired me to write a history of the present. The emergence of a new generation of activists in groups such as Black Lives Matter (BLM), Black Youth Project 100 (BYP100), Assata's Daughters, Lost Voices, Hands Up United, Dream Defenders, and many, many others echoed historical developments that I had so carefully excavated from the preceding half century. Mass protests in Ferguson, Missouri, Baltimore, Maryland, and Charlotte, North Carolina, drew me to write about contemporary politics for the first time, as they spoke directly to the history of resistance I unearthed in my previous scholarship on postwar Black Radicalism.[5]

Today, the mass mobilization of protest following the killings of Breonna Taylor and George Floyd has opened up a national dialogue on prison abolition, structural racism, and defunding the police that would have been unimaginable just a few years before. Looking back at those years of constant political struggle and growth from 2012 through 2016, it is striking how foundational they were for the explosion of protest at the height of the COVID-19 crisis of 2020. Two different threads from this genesis period for BLMM/M4BL carried through to the era of mass uprisings in the spring and summer of 2020, when the United States witnessed the largest protest movement in its history.[6] New political networks, organizations, and activists made up the first, while the second unfolded in the larger realm of ideas and common sense. The articulation of Black Lives Matter provided a powerful challenge to flagrant white supremacy and indifference to the loss of life itself that reached its apex under the Trump administration.

Throughout modern US history, the mainstream media, law enforcement, and politicians in both parties have deployed a constant barrage of racial tropes to justify the enormous expenditures on law enforcement and its accompanying wars on crime, drugs, and gangs.

Be it the "superpredator" or the "crack mother," as political theorist Stuart Hall argued, the spectacle of dangerous "others" obscured the expanded scale of policing and incarceration by demonizing vulnerable populations. As this punitive turn unfolded, a steady gutting of social services, public goods, and reversals of the social protections of the New Deal led to the rapid downward mobility of large segments of the population. Bipartisan support for a punishing state stripped of social welfare protections has been core to American politics since the early 1970s, resulting in an unprecedented number of incarcerated people and swollen police budgets that form the largest line item of many cities' expenditures.[7]

Until the rise of BLMM/M4BL, the hegemony of law and order appeared unassailable. However, by politicizing police killings of Black people, this movement successfully reframed the race to punishment as an assault on Black life, thereby redirecting the locus of threat from criminalized populations of color to state violence itself. This conceptual shift included the immediacy of police murders, as well as the protracted web of harassment, arbitrary arrest, cash bail, incarceration, and criminal legal obligations discussed in chapter 7, "Paying for Punishment." Many activists began advocating for structural changes rather than marginal reform of the multitiered carceral system at the local, county, state, and federal levels. "Some were embracing the politics of abolition and the belief that society would be better off without the entire carceral paradigm," historian Keeanga-Yamahtta Taylor explained five years after the Ferguson rebellions. "Instead of spending $80 billion a year to put human beings in cages, maybe those resources could be redistributed in such a way as to make people's lives better instead of being used to punish."[8]

In the aftermath of George Floyd's violent suffocation by police on May 25, 2020, activists gained notoriety for their demands to abolish the police, but before that, they had been politicized in the previous decade through protesting the killings of Jamar Clark and other Black residents. Local protests amplified the call to "defund the police," as shorthand for a sweeping reassessment of governance in which the only way to truly halt the punitive carceral regime was to redirect police budgets toward much-needed social services. One of the most important contributions of the BLMM/M4BL movement has been providing a moral framework to move beyond the narrow agenda of criminal justice reform, and instead, to fight for transformative change. Kandace Montgomery of Minneapolis's Black Visions Collective occupied a police station in North Minneapolis for eighteen days after police killed Jamar Clark. She went on to cofound Black Visions Collective in 2017, and the following year, Reclaim the Block, which used grassroots and city council organizing to redirect monies from police to "community health and safety." Anishinaabe activist Arianna Nason of the Fond du Lac Band of Lake Superior Chippewa stressed that their organizing efforts in the years after the Ferguson rebellion directly informed activist work to dismantle the carceral state during the George Floyd protests in 2020. "The seeds around abolition had been planted," Nason explained, "but the season of harvest had to be right, and I think that's where we are now."[9]

It is in this context that the emergence of mainstream debate over the "defund the police" slogan should be understood. According to the Kaiser Family Foundation, pollsters found that one in every ten adults they surveyed identified themselves as participants in BLMM/M4BL demonstrations in 2020. Under the pressures of the COVID-19 era, in which mandatory shutdown orders devastated the economy, with poor and working-class people subjected to Depression-era levels of unemployment, millions took to the streets. These protests reached their apex on June 6, 2020, when five hundred thousand people joined uprisings in more than 550 locations throughout the United States. Mass protest in support of Black lives prompted the mainstream media's discussion of "structural racism" and abolitionist demands to defund the police that would have been unimaginable a decade before. The

nied them. Mass rebellion and organizing against state violence and racial capitalism animates this book's final chapters, as does the wisdom of Assata Shakur, who reminds us that "dreams and reality are opposites" if not synthesized by action.[12]

PART I

BLACK POWER AND BLACK RADICALISM

CHAPTER 1

The Campus and the Street

Race, Migration, and the Origins of the Black Panther Party in Oakland, California

The great exodus of poor people out of the South during World War II sprang from the hope for a better life in the big cities of the North and West. In search of freedom, they left behind centuries of Southern cruelty and repression. The futility of that search is now history. The Black communities of Bedford-Stuyvesant, Newark, Brownsville, Watts, Detroit, and many others stand as testament that racism is as oppressive in the North as in the South. Oakland is no different.

—Huey Newton[1]

n 1948 Harry Haywood wrote, "The Negro Question is agrarian in origin. . . . It presents the curious anomaly of a virtual serfdom in the very heart of the most highly industrialized country in the world."[2] World War II and the advent of the mechanical cotton picker resolved this contradiction by spurring the single largest Black population movement in US history. In an ever-expanding tide, migrants poured out of the South in pursuit of rising wages and living standards promised by

---

* "The Campus and the Street: Race, Migration, and the Origins of the Black Panther Party in Oakland, CA" originally appeared in *Souls* IX, no. 4 (2007). Taylor & Francis Ltd. Reprinted with permission.

major metropolitan areas. In 1940, 77 percent of the total Black population lived in the South with over 49 percent in rural areas; two out of
five worked as farmers, sharecroppers, or farm laborers. In the next ten
years, over 1.6 million Black people migrated north and westward, to be
followed by another 1.5 million in the subsequent decade.[3]

The repercussions of this internal migration were felt throughout
the United States, leaving their deepest imprint on West Coast cities
that historically possessed small Black populations. California's lucrative defense industries made the state a prime destination for Southern
migrants. By 1943, the San Francisco Chamber of Commerce declared
the Bay Area "the largest shipbuilding center in the world."[4] Sociologist
Charles Johnson explained, "To the romantic appeal of the west, has
been added the real and actual opportunity for gainful employment,
setting in motion a wartime migration of huge proportions."[5] Oakland's
Black population mushroomed from 8,462 residents in 1940 (3 percent) to an impressive 47,562 in 1950 (12 percent).[6] A pattern of chain
migration continued until 1980, when Oakland reached the racial tip-
ping point with 157,484 Black residents, 51 percent of the city's total.[7]
The resulting shift in demography secured Oakland's position as the
largest Black metropolis in northern California.

In the two decades following World War II, Oakland's recently
settled African American community produced one of the most influential local Black Power movements in the country.[8] First- and sec-
ond-generation migrants who came of age in the late 1950s and early
1960s composed not only the leadership, but also the rank and file
of large segments of the Black Panther Party (BPP) and other Black
Power organizations.[9] In contrast to their parents who entered the San
Francisco Bay Area in a time of economic boom, postwar youth faced a
rapidly disappearing industrial base along with increased school, neighborhood, and job segregation. However, socioeconomic factors alone
cannot explain the development of Bay Area radicalism. In response
to the rapidly growing (and disproportionately young) migrant pop-

ulation, city and state governments developed a program to combat "juvenile delinquency" that resulted in high rates of police harassment, arrest, and incarceration.[10] With its founding in October of 1966, the Black Panther Party for Self-Defense (BPPSD) mobilized against this new scale of repression by organizing young people throughout the Bay Area. Within a few short years, the Oakland-based group dropped the words "Self Defense" from its name and expanded into an international force with chapters in over sixty-one US cities and twenty-six states.[11]

Although the BPPSD is best known for its armed police patrols and embrace of "brothers off the block" as revolutionary vanguard, this essay argues that its origins lay in Black student and campus struggles at Merritt College and UC Berkeley. While we often think of Black Studies as the product rather than the catalyst of postwar social movements, in the Bay Area fights over curriculum and hiring in the early 1960s were integral to the emergence of Black Power after Watts. Radical groups like the Panthers reflected not only the problems, but the ambitions of California's migrant communities who saw schooling as "the primary vehicle for their children's upward mobility."[12] Oral testimony reveals that for many Black families greater educational access helped inspire western migration itself. Melvyn Newton, brother of the Panther cofounder Huey Newton, expressed this sentiment most clearly. "We were children of migrants that came here for social opportunity . . . families . . . came with the dream of sending their kids to school. I don't know if they necessarily knew what schools were like out here, but they knew what the conditions were like out there."[13] Given the postindustrial restructuring of Oakland's economy and penal system, the need for quality education took on a particular urgency.

BLACK MIGRATION AND WORLD WAR II

Prior to World War II, the Black community of the San Francisco Bay Area was tiny. In the first quarter of the century, Black residents actively discouraged migration because of limited economic opportunity. World War II ushered in a new era; national defense brought in unprecedented policy and capital investment in the state. The federal government invested over $40 billion in West Coast factories, military bases, and other capital improvements. The resulting economic and demographic changes to the region were immense.[14] In 1943, the *San Francisco Chronicle* summed up this process by announcing that "the Second Gold Rush" had begun.[15] While people fled from regions throughout the South, and brought with them a diversity of experiences and backgrounds, Bay Area war migrants shared some particular characteristics. The majority came from Texas, Louisiana, and Oklahoma, with Arkansas and Mississippi contributing lesser numbers.[16] With an average age between twenty-two and twenty-three, they were younger than the resident population and disproportionately female.[17]

In addition to the obvious economic incentives, the San Francisco Bay Area held a special allure for these young migrants. Racial segregation functioned like a palimpsest whose layers grew denser with the passage of time. The recent migration of the East Bay's Black community meant that prior to the population influx spurred by World War II, formal systems of racial control had not yet been consolidated. Black rates of property ownership in California ranked among the highest in the nation, and in contrast to their places of origin, Black migrants suffered less physical repression, worked largely outside agriculture, and had greater access to public services.[18] Most importantly, the state's promise of higher quality public education at all levels tapped a persistent, if understudied, motive for Black migration throughout the twentieth century.[19]

By 1945, national defense industries had produced more than six hundred thousand jobs for African Americans and drawn a million Black Southerners to northern and western industrial centers. Although Bay Area shipyards resisted hiring Black workers at the outset of the War, systematic organizing efforts by C. L. Dellums, the local business agent for the Brotherhood of Sleeping Car Porters, and other Civil Rights leaders forced both unions and local employers to hire African Americans.[20] Their campaign provided this newly settled population with unprecedented economic opportunity. In the Bay Area, over 70 percent of Black migrants found work in the shipyards, and Black female employment tripled.[21] Southern migration combined with a changing job structure inaugurated the formation of a strong Black working-class movement. C. L. Dellums, a close friend of A. Philip Randolph and uncle to future congressman Ronald Dellums, remained a touchstone of local Black politics in subsequent decades, and his union became one of the most powerful Black institutions in the East Bay. However, this era of abundance proved fleeting as postwar demobilization led to large-scale unemployment and economic uncertainty.[22]

DEINDUSTRIALIZATION

As migrants sought to realize their newfound opportunity, a new and more repressive racial order emerged. African Americans who had fled the poverty and brutality of the South soon found new barriers erected upon arrival. In 1946, the Final Report of the Fair Employment Practices Committee argued that "the entire West Coast Area is characterized by problems which in newness and intensity distinguish it from the rest of the country."[23] Black labor's remarkable gains quickly receded. The workforce employed by shipbuilders shrank from two hundred and fifty thousand at the War's height to twelve thousand people in 1946.[24] In Oakland and south Berkeley, five short years of boom were followed by long decades of bust. Immediately after the War ended, Oakland entered a period of industrial decline, and structural unemployment became a permanent feature of the local economy. By 1960, the federal government officially classified Oakland as a depressed area.[25] Despite California's thriving Cold War economy, Oakland limped along. Deindustrialization had a devastating social impact on African American residents. In 1959, one-quarter of the total population in Oakland lived under the poverty line and roughly 10 percent earned less than $2,000 per year.[26] Union discrimination, concentration in temporary wartime industry like shipyards, and entrenched patterns of employer discrimination relegated much of the growing Black population to secondary labor markets. Black youth remained most vulnerable to economic retrenchment, facing high rates of unemployment and repression from local law enforcement.[27]

POLICE REPRESSION AND "JUVENILE DELINQUENCY"

Among historians, it is well recognized that white residential and capital flight from cities was a direct reaction to Black migration. In Oakland and other metropolitan areas in California, however, city and state government's postwar preoccupation with "juvenile delinquency" was an equally important development. Racial anxieties about the city's rapidly changing demographics led to an increasing integration of school and recreational programs with police and penal authorities. In this context, the discourse of "juvenile delinquency" took on a clear racial caste, leading to wide-scale policing and criminalization of Black youth. While extensive police harassment and arrest of Black migrants started during the population influx of World War II, it vastly intensified in the period of economic decline that ensued.[28]

In the 1950s, public service agencies fielded the cascade of disputes that followed from Black settlement in white enclaves. School grounds and recreation areas became volatile flashpoints of racial conflict. White neighborhoods undergoing swift racial transition sought to obtain funds from the city council to reorganize social service agencies. When city government refused to allocate money for specific areas, groups of residents banded together to form the Associated Agencies (AA) and District Community Councils (DCA).[29] In its final form, the AA of Oakland encompassed three tiers of government responsible for youth and family services. At the local level, the AA integrated Oakland's public school system, recreation, and police departments with the county's probation, welfare, and health agencies. In turn, these local groups were linked up with the California Youth Authority, the state's largest penal authority for juvenile offenders.[30] Meetings with multiple family service and juvenile agencies allowed them to work together to identify and monitor "troublemakers."[31] The most disturbing aspect of this integration of recreational and police agencies was the tracking of youths identified as delinquent. Police monitored, and even arrested, individuals that had been identified by school and recreational staff, despite the fact that they had no prior record. Increasingly, the category of Black youth itself became defined as a social problem at best, and as a criminal presence at worst.

Local politicians used Cold War metaphors of contagion and containment to describe Black residents, with the greatest threat emanating from the youth. Oakland city manager Wayne Thompson, a self-professed liberal, explained the preventative logic behind introducing police and penal presence into the local school system to stem the tide of "delinquency." "If you didn't stop it, it would spread into the business sections and even infect the industrial community," Thompson warned. "We had eyes and ears in those areas to alert us in advance. . . . Before the Associated Agencies program, it was an admission of weakness on the part of the school official, or . . . failure if he even let a policeman in the door. . . . What a change now! The first man they call is the police.[32]

In the mid-1950s, a restructuring of the Oakland Police Department (OPD) exacerbated this situation. Changes in East Bay law enforcement reflected a national trend toward "legalistic policing," characterized by modern equipment, formalized systems, and greater emphasis on juvenile detention. Oakland's new police chief dissolved local precincts, concentrated the OPD into a single headquarters, and overhauled hiring practices in favor of better educated, more affluent candidates.[33] In practice, these policies created an almost exclusively white middle-class force that resided outside the city and had little understanding or connection to the neighborhoods they served.[34] Oakland's reinvigorated police force became a constant and intrusive presence in people's lives. Systematic arrests of young offenders linked them into the web of professional services, including probation officers, judges, and child guidance clinics, further blurring the line between "authoritative" police functions and family services.[35] Given the pervasive hostility toward Black migrants, this framework laid the basis for the simultaneous criminalization of Black youth and long-term neglect of Black families.

BLACK STUDENTS AND THE ROOTS OF BLACK POWER

While Black Power has often been treated as a post-Watts phenomenon, its roots in the East Bay stretch far back into the decade preceding the urban rebellions.[36] Public education became the most immediate arena in which migrant youth confronted a hostile white establishment and mobilized against it.[37] Black students entered secondary schools and universities in large numbers at a time when the California system of higher education was undergoing a major restructuring. Faced with a mushrooming population and a conservative fiscal structure, state policy makers sought to contain costs while expanding capacity. Projections warned that student populations would increase nearly fivefold in fifteen years. In 1960, 227,000 students were enrolled in higher education, by 1975, the total reached 1 million.[38] California's university system, with its integrated tiers of community colleges, state, and public universities, led the nation in superior levels of funding, infrastructure, and quality of instruction.

In 1960, the statewide Master Plan for Higher Education vastly increased the number and capacity of junior colleges and mandated that they admit all applicants with high school diplomas. Urban campuses greatly expanded college enrollment of Black working-class people, and provided an institutional base for political organizing. By 1969, the San Francisco Bay Area boasted one of the highest rates of minority college completion in the nation.[39] Full access to community colleges became particularly important given racial segregation and inequalities in the city's primary and secondary schools.

The Oakland Unified School District consistently allocated resources to segregated white schools in wealthy areas of the city, while neglecting overcrowded schools in the "flatlands." In the early sixties, this issue came to a head with the building of Skyline High School in the Oakland hills. Black parents and Civil Rights leaders charged the school board with "gerrymandering" the district and draining resources from the rapidly integrating schools in the low-lying areas of the city. Discrimination extended beyond issues of unfair financing to the racialized culture of the schools themselves. Starting in 1957, Black students and their families protested low standards and achievements in West Oakland's all-Black McClymonds High School. They cited the low rate of college attendance among "Mack" graduates, and a recurring pattern of counselors and school officials discouraging students from continuing their education.[40] A Fair Employment Practices Committee report published several years later identified differential standards as a pervasive problem throughout the district. Principals and teachers in majority-Black schools repeatedly emphasized the importance of discipline, comportment, and hygiene over academic achievement.[41] In the spring of 1966, the Ad Hoc Committee for Quality Education (AHCQUE) formed to protest the school board's unfair use of resources and the school's miseducation of their children.[42] Over the next decade, flatland parents and their supporters vigorously contested the increased police presence in the schools, the failure to hire Black faculty and staff, and the self-fulfilling prophecy of lowered expectations producing poor academic results.

DONALD WARDEN AND THE AFRO-AMERICAN ASSOCIATION

In the San Francisco Bay Area, some of the most important battles over curriculum and social access took place at the university level. In under a decade, unprecedented numbers of Black students entered college for the first time, and urban campuses became major sites for political organizing. In the spring of 1961, Berkeley graduate students from a variety of disciplines and a sprinkling of undergraduates from UC Berkeley and San Francisco State began to meet regularly. Donald Warden, a second-year student at UC Berkeley's Boalt School of Law, emerged as the "leader" of the study group. In early March, he wrote a series of editorials to the *Daily California*, denouncing Roy Wilkins, the NAACP, and the Civil Rights strategy of integration.[43] Students debated books of immediate political relevance and hosted weekly forums throughout the Bay Area. Charter members included Henry Ramsey, Donald Hopkins, Ann Cooke, Mary Lewis, and Maurice Dawson.[44] As the group cohered, they chose the name Afro-American Association (AAA) and limited membership exclusively to people of African descent.[45] Ernest Allen, a Merritt student who later joined, described the choice as containing a "revolutionary . . . sense of rebirth" paralleling the Nation of Islam's repudiation of "slave names."[46] W. E. B. Du Bois's *Souls of Black Folk*, Carter G. Woodson's *Miseducation of the Negro*, and Ralph Ellison's *Invisible Man* numbered among their selections; however, E. Franklin Frazier's *Black Bourgeoisie* and Melville J. Herskovits's *The Myth of the Negro Past* elicited the most debate.[47] The discussion and the controversy these two volumes engendered had the greatest impact on the Association's evolving ideology. Ultimately, the Afro-American Association successfully fused Herskovits's and Frazier's opposing views on African survivals to fashion its own anti-assimilationist ideology.[48]

Many of the ideas generated in the Association, including their debates about the nature of identity, African retention, and the integrationist sins of the Black middle class, anticipated cultural nationalist thought of subsequent years.[49] In May of 1961, Association members worked together with the UC Berkeley campus chapter of the NAACP to bring Malcolm X to speak. Soon after, a group of students began regularly attending the Nation of Islam's mosque, Temple 26B, in West Oakland. Although the Association remained secular, their rhetoric revealed the Nation of Islam's clear influence.[50] Opposition to integration, understood as forced assimilation, served as the unifying theme; their public speeches often reserved their greatest rancor not for the dominant white society as for the compliant "Black Bourgeoisie." Warden and others in the Association argued that while Civil Rights leaders spoke of desegregation and compliance with Brown, what they truly advocated was assimilation. They encouraged their members to learn Arabic and Swahili, and in the mid-sixties began manufacturing an African-inspired garment called the "Simba."[51] Ronald Everett, later known as Ronald Karenga (founder of the Black nationalist US organization), joined the Association in 1963 and helped establish a Los Angeles chapter of the AAA. Historian Scot Brown notes that "Warden, though not specifically defining the group as cultural nationalist, set in motion many of the cultural concepts and organizing principles that Karenga utilized in US."[52]

The Afro-American Association was not content to simply remain a study group; Warden and others moved on to become integral to the East Bay's larger African American community. Association members experimented with different forms of activism, including sponsoring the "Mind of the Ghetto" youth conference at McClymonds High in West Oakland. However, Harlem-style street rallies remained the AAA's most consistent form of outreach.[53] Although street speaking had long been a staple of Black nationalist political culture, the Afro-American Association adapted it to the particularities of the Bay Area. A pattern developed in which the Association held rallies in San Francisco until early afternoon, before moving on to Oakland and to Richmond. The exile of Black self-defense activist Robert F. Williams prompted one of the first street speaking sessions. Association members traveled down to 7th Street, the central Black business district in West Oakland, and held up the newspaper headlines, loudly proclaiming their support.[54] Looking back, Maurice Dawson remembered the uproar over Williams's exile as a turning point. The name Robert F. Williams was poised on everyone's lips. "[He] ain't scared of nothing or nobody," Dawson explained. "This was the talk of the Bay Area. . . . It was the genesis of the growth and evolution, frankly, of racial pride in the East Bay."[55]

In early 1963, the Afro-American Association reached the height of its powers and influence. The Association offered an effective mix of Black cultural nationalism and colorful display that helped mobilize a whole generation that passed through Bay Area schools. The support the Association received from different segments of the Black community reflected its profound appeal. Many participants in the Association later became prominent across a broad spectrum of Black politics. On the electoral front, Ronald Dellums briefly attended meetings along with future Oakland mayor Elihu Harris and local powerbrokers Ortho Green, Henry Ramsey, and Donald Hopkins. Charter member Ann Cooke went on to publish in the groundbreaking feminist anthology *The Black Woman*, while political radicals Ernest Allen, Cedric Robinson, Huey Newton, and Bobby Seale socialized with nationalists Ronald Karenga, Fritz Pointer, and David Patterson.[56] In sum, the Association represented a foundational stage in the evolution of Black politics in California. While an older school of historiography has emphasized the divisions between Civil Rights and electoral politics on the one hand, and Black nationalist and Black

Power thought on the other, the history of the Afro-American Association clearly demonstrates how the two were nurtured together in this
early student movement.

Despite the Association's many accomplishments, this period of
unity was short-lived. The AAA soon underwent a series of splits that
alienated a core portion of its more radical membership. Students interested in socialism and direct community action became frustrated
by Warden's recalcitrant anti-communism and his resistance to more
concrete forms of political organizing. Others questioned his political
integrity and personal motivation.[57] Nevertheless, the Afro-American
Association helped launch a new era of Black activism and institution
building that culminated in the founding of the Black Panther Party
for Self-Defense.

MERRITT COLLEGE, BLACK STUDIES, AND THE BLACK PANTHER PARTY

While the Afro-American Association recruited throughout the East
Bay, its largest following emerged at Merritt College, affectionately
known to Black residents as "Grove Street." Ernest Allen explained,
"The fact that it [Merritt College] was located right in the middle of a
community was a historical accident, but what people made of it was
something else."[58] The boundary between Merritt and North Oakland
was completely porous. People passed on and off the campus, and
many residents from the surrounding area hung out in the cafeteria,
a major hub for debate.[59] By locating its headquarters adjacent to the
school and regularly staging street rallies on campus grounds, the Association helped ignite a militant Black student movement.

Until the late fifties, African American presence on California
campuses was too small and diffuse to be called a community. Although the University of California did not collect statistics on the
racial breakdown of the Berkeley student population until 1966,
anecdotal evidence reveals that there were fewer than one hundred

Black students out of nearly twenty thousand. As the Civil Rights Movement progressed these figures began to slowly increase, until by 1966, Black students, including both native born and African, breached the 1 percent barrier with 226 undergraduate and graduate students enrolled in Berkeley.[60]

Although these gains were significant, the expansion of the Black student body at community colleges dwarfed that of the comparatively elite University of California system. By 1965 Black students made up nearly 10 percent of Merritt College's total enrollment, and within two short years, they formed over 30 percent of the student body. A mutually reinforcing dynamic took hold in which the increase in Black students fed political organizing, and political organizing, in turn, attracted people who would never have considered attending college.[61]

Many of these students were not only the first members of their family to attend college, but they were also recent arrivals from the South who still retained strong cultural ties to their families' places of origin. Their intermediary status as migrants led them to look "backwards as much as forwards" and helped to provide additional motivation for seizing opportunities unimaginable to them and their families a decade before.[62] While Huey Newton was exceptional in many ways, his background typified that of the growing Black student body at Merritt College. He was the child of Louisiana migrants, raised in poverty in Oakland by parents who had come to California in search of better jobs and more educational opportunity. Similarly, Bobby Seale was a first-generation migrant from Dallas, Texas.[63] In the late 1950s, Seale began taking night classes at Merritt with hopes of earning a degree in engineering. As his interest in "American Black History" grew, he shifted his emphasis from technical training toward the humanities.[64] Attending community college was the single biggest influence on their radicalization, Newton later explained. "It was my studying and reading in college that led me to become a socialist.

... The transformation from a nationalist to a socialist was a slow one, although I was around a lot of Marxists."[65]

In the mid-1960s, Merritt students began organizing to have Black Studies classes included in the regular curriculum. Between 1964 and 1966, Virtual Murrell, Alex Papillion, Isaac Moore, Kenny Freeman, Ernest Allen, and Douglas Allen formed the Soul Students Advisory Council (SSAC).[66] Leo Bazile, who became president of SSAC in 1966, described the organization as a place where "youth met and devised political involvements." The same year they changed their name to "Black Student Union," a new term at the time. One of the Council's first accomplishments was a large rally at Merritt protesting the draft of Blacks into the military. However, their fight to implement Black history classes at Merritt and to increase the hiring of Black faculty and staff became their most sustained campaign.[67]

After a confrontation with white faculty member Rodney Carlisle over the content of his "Negro History" class, Huey Newton became involved in this protracted struggle.[68] He saw it as an important chance to implement a new type of organizing. Newton proposed sponsoring a rally in support of the Afro-American History Program in which SSAC members would invite the press, strap on guns, and march outside Merritt College on Malcolm X's birthday. This type of action would enable Soul Students to mobilize not only students, but the populations surrounding the school, including the "lumpen proletariat," the key constituency for social revolution.[69] A display of armed self-defense would impress the community, call attention to police brutality, and intimidate Merritt's administrators into taking the students' demands more seriously.[70] Soul Students refused, and Newton refocused his attention on the world beyond the "the sandbox politics" of the community college.

While the Black Panther Party had its origins firmly in early student activism at Berkeley and Merritt College, Seale and Newton quickly distanced themselves from their campus roots and cultivated their image as "brothers off the block." Newton viewed the gun as a powerful "recruiting device" that would attract youth from the broader community, thereby bridging the gap between students and the grassroots. This duality, merging different strata from "college and community," remained a hallmark of the Black Panther Party throughout its history. Given the sharp spike in local college attendance, this dynamic was strongest in Oakland, but it was true for other chapters as well. In describing the Chicago chapter, David Hilliard likened its strategy to Bunchy Carter's efforts in Los Angeles: "They [tried] to forge an alliance between the two largest concentrations of Black youth—the campus and the streets."[71]

While many Black nationalist and New Left groups hoped to do this, the Panthers set about achieving this broad coalition through spectacular displays challenging state violence. As Newton searched for a medium to "capture the imagination" of Oakland's Black community, he turned to the law library at the North Oakland Neighborhood Anti-Poverty Center, a poverty program that employed Bobby Seale. Drawing on his training from law school, Newton pored over the California penal code and resurrected an old statute that legalized carrying unconcealed weapons. After much discussion with peers over the right to bear arms, Newton and Seale decided that they needed a concrete political program before initiating police patrols. In October 1966, in less than twenty minutes, Seale and Newton drafted the "Black Panther Party Platform and Program" in the North Oakland Neighborhood Anti-Poverty Center.[72]

One of the Panthers' first community actions took place on 55th and Market near the anti-poverty program where Newton and Seale were working. Several pedestrians had been killed at the intersection, which had no stoplight. They had attempted to get the city to put up a stop sign and made little progress with local bureaucracy, so they went out and started directing traffic; within weeks, the city installed a signal. This strategy of forcing the hand of local government through assuming some of its powers was repeated a number of times throughout the Party's history.[73] Policing the police, food giveaways, and public service actions like the one on Market highlighted the simultaneously negligent and repressive role of government in Oakland's Black neighborhoods. The implicit message was clear—either improve state services or face an armed movement of local youth.

CONCLUSION

Ultimately, Oakland's Black Power Movement is best understood through the historical circumstances that produced it. Large-scale migration to California, impelled first by defense industry and the inertia of chain migration—and later by the death throes of agricultural tenancy—created a displaced population that remained shut out of the major avenues of decision-making. For first-generation migrants, shipyard and defense-related employment promised a vast increase in living standards that quickly dissolved in the war's aftermath. As jobs and money flowed to the suburbs in coming decades, the core of the migrant population found itself trapped in the familiar cycles of poverty and debt. For the young, the situation was most difficult of all because they not only faced economic uncertainty but also the constant threat of police harassment and incarceration. As they approached college age, federal funding and an expansive network of community colleges provided newfound access to integrated higher education. Black students seized this opportunity, and used it as an arena for addressing the most immediate circumstances of their lives. College campuses became major sites for political organizing, and first-generation attendees articulated the grievances of the larger community. Black Studies and student union struggles created strong networks of activists that would later venture beyond the campus into grassroots and community organizing after 1965. The Afro-American Association, US Organization, and the Black Panther

Party all had origins in these campus-based struggles. Huey Newton said it best: "Everyone—from Warden and the Afro-American Association to Malcolm X and the Muslims to all the other groups active in the Bay Area at that time—believed strongly that the failure to include Black history in the college curriculum was a scandal. We all set out to do something about it."[74]

CHAPTER 2

BLACK LIBERATION AND 1968

My assessment of 1968 fifty years later is inseparable from my own particulars of time and place. The fateful year that witnessed the Tet Offensive, the Black Power Olympic protests, and the successive assassinations of Martin Luther King Jr. and Bobby Kennedy happened also to be the year of my birth. As a result, I view the events as only someone from a subsequent generation could, with the distance of received knowledge, but also with a sense of recognition. Given my father's activism in St. Louis CORE and the ever-present talk about Nixon, the antiwar movement, and Black Liberation politics in our home, I always felt that researching the late sixties was like trying to recall the lyrics from a familiar melody whose words you never quite knew.

Attending the University of California, Berkeley, for graduate school in the late 1990s and early 2000s also informs my view of this pivotal year. Reconstructing the postwar history of the East Bay's Black radical movement as a doctoral student during the George W. Bush years gave me an intimate knowledge of one of the most important sites of radical struggle in the late 1960s. At the time, what was most striking to me was not the school's unbroken continuity with "Berkeley in the Sixties," but rather the university's rupture with its activist past, precisely because of its pivotal role as a battleground for the Cold War and the international Black freedom struggle. By

---

* "Black Liberation and 1968" first appeared in *American Historical Review* 123, no. 3 (June 2018): 717–21, https://doi.org/10.1093/ahr/123.3.717.

the mid-nineties, Berkeley and the elite campuses of the University of California system more broadly had become a staging ground for backlash against affirmative action, equality of opportunity, and radical ethnic studies.

For professional historians, the choice of a single year is often an argument about causation or periodization, while for popular audiences, the choice of a fixed moment in time is almost always symbolic of a larger meaning, zeitgeist, or sensibility. The global essence of 1968 evoked a mass revolt of the young fed by the expansion of higher education, a doubling of the university student population worldwide, and the postwar baby boom. Demographic change intermeshed with the global repercussions of decolonization as young people from the industrialized economies of the North drew inspiration from anticolonial and nationalist struggles in Vietnam, Congo, Cuba, and other political theaters of the Global South.[1]

This history was nowhere more evident in the United States than in the founding of the Black Panther Party for Self-Defense in Oakland, California, in 1966. Born at the nexus of the Second Great Migration and the explosion of youth revolt on college campuses, the Black Panther Party (BPP) took form just fifteen minutes south of the UC Berkeley campus. The new organization extended back to the early sixties, when a group of Berkeley graduate and undergraduate students formed the first Black nationalist study group in California, the Afro-American Association. Mobilized by the murder of Patrice Lumumba in Congo, the growing prominence of Malcolm X, and the scores of independence struggles sweeping the African continent, a cohort of Black students, drawn first from the UC campus and later from Merritt College and other regional community colleges, came together to debate the meaning of color and nation.[2] While they repudiated their cultural nationalist predecessors, the Panthers played a definitive role in shaping student protest throughout California's public colleges. They sold Mao's Little Red Book on the UC campus to raise money for their burgeoning organization, and Berkeley's thriving antiwar movement proved fertile soil for interracial coalition with "mother country radicals," who adamantly opposed Cold War intervention in Southeast Asia. Indeed, the BPP's internationalism and embrace first of internal colonization, and later of intercommunalism can be understood only in the context of its pragmatic, multiracial, anticolonial alliances. Tellingly, in 1968, the Peace and Freedom Party nominated Eldridge Cleaver as its presidential candidate even though he was several months shy of the required age minimum of thirty-five.

The history of 1968 and Black Liberation has gone through two major revisions, which reflect a shift from a backlash analysis centered on the electoral realignment of white Democratic voters with the Republican Party to a much more expansive, and sympathetic, understanding of the Black freedom struggle. Throughout my years in graduate school during the Clinton and Bush years, 1968 served as the linchpin of a declensionist narrative of "the good sixties vs. the bad sixties." This antimony mourned the loss of a "beloved community" of interracial struggle defeated by the rise of Black Power and its bête noir, the Black Panther Party. Emphasis on great men and charismatic leadership helped to reinforce this narrative by making the deaths of King and Kennedy definitive tragedies with cataclysmic consequences for American democracy. In numerous respects, this narrative proved faulty. Despite 1968's powerful political symbolism, the periodization of the postwar Black radical movement fits uncomfortably within its fixed temporal framework. The passage of the Voting Rights Act three years before, the explosion of the Watts rebellion in August 1965, the election of Stokely Carmichael to the leadership of the Student Nonviolent Coordinating Committee in June 1966, and the formation of the BPP in October of the same year all highlight the importance of the years prior. In this sense, 1968 has become more a synecdoche of a particular type of politics than an organic product of events.

Although Berkeley in the sixties figured large in people's historical imagination, its campus and the larger San Francisco Bay Area
also nurtured some of the staunchest opposition to sixties youth
radicalism. In the decades that followed, the history of the BPP and
the radical student movement haunted the UC Berkeley campus
in myriad ways. Its ghosts were everywhere, from the talk of Huey
Newton's application to the History Department in the 1970s, to
the whispers about political science professors who had been pro-
moted for their steadfast opposition to the free speech movement
in the ensuing years. To some extent, Berkeley had buttressed itself
from the student revolt, and by the 1990s the University of California system had actually become a major staging ground in the attack
on affirmative action rooted in the Bakke decision in 1978, the Regents' decision to eliminate race-based admissions in 1995, and the
subsequent co-authorship of the California Civil Rights Initiative by
Boalt Law School professor John Yoo. Prior to coming to Berkeley,
Yoo had clerked for Supreme Court justice Clarence Thomas, and
he would later become infamous for his authorship of the *Torture
Memos* supporting enhanced interrogation techniques such as wa-
terboarding during the Iraq War.[3]

National figures with historical connections to the Bay Area, such
as Todd Gitlin, former head of the Students for a Democratic Society,
who had also witnessed the San Francisco State strike firsthand, later
condemned Black Power politics by name as well as through the capacious abstraction of "identity politics."[4] David Horowitz, who also
had deep Bay Area roots as a former BPP fellow traveler who helped
to establish the Panthers' Oakland Community School as a not-for-
profit, subsequently made an abrupt about-face in the years after the
party's demise. He went on to weaponize this argument for the racist
right by taking devolution one step further, claiming not only that the
Panther Party had damaged the interracial coalition, but that from its
inception, the group had always been a murderous antiwhite criminal

organization. In response, several generations of African American historians have worked to debunk the declensionist narrative of the late sixties, and by implication to reframe the importance of Black Liberation and Black Power as part of a longer historical arc reaching back to the Popular Front and World War II.[5]

Ultimately, the declensionist narrative itself naturalized the intensified half-century-long War on Crime by identifying Black radicals as the cause rather than the victims of state repression. While the mid- to late sixties marked a significant shift toward state repression in the domestic US, as the work of Elizabeth Hinton, Heather Thompson, and others has shown, this is best understood through refocusing attention on the expanding carceral apparatus of prisons, policing, surveillance, and punishment. In reassessing 1968 from a half century of hindsight, what is most striking is how definitive the year was for the criminalization of radical Black protest, ranging from the punitive attack on urban rebellions that swept the country after King's assassination to the targeted assaults on the segment of the Black Liberation movement that confronted domestic racial violence through the lens of state socialism and anticolonial struggle. In November 1968, FBI director J. Edgar Hoover declared the Black Panther Party to be the single "greatest threat to the internal security of the country," thereby unleashing a virulent campaign against the organization just as it had begun to turn toward community survival programs. Strikingly, between 1968 and 1969, the Black Panther newspaper reported that police had arrested 739 people nationwide, with the BPP subsequently paying nearly $5 million in bail.[6]

Although 1968 certainly was not the starting point for escalating police powers, the federal government's draconian response to urban unrest, followed by Richard Nixon's subsequent election on a law-and-order platform, represented a definitive moment in the history of racialized mass incarceration. Starting in the early 1960s, during the seismic shifts of the Southern Civil Rights Movement and the

Second Great Migration, the federal government began incremental-
ly constructing the "architecture of criminalization" that would have
devastating effects for Black populations in the years to come. From
John F. Kennedy's passage of the Juvenile Delinquency and Youth
Offenses Control Act of 1961 through Lyndon Johnson's simultaneous declaration of a War on Poverty and a War on Crime, the legislative agenda hinged on assumptions about the pathological nature
of Black urban populations. This bipartisan punishment campaign
culminated in the passage of the Omnibus Crime Control and Safe
Streets Act of 1968, which provided $400 million in "seed money"
to expand law enforcement efforts across the country. It established
the Law Enforcement Assistance Administration, which became the
"fastest-growing federal agency" of the 1970s, with a budget that
mushroomed from $10 million at its inception to $850 million in
1973.[7] Significantly, a Democratic administration provided Richard
Nixon with all the tools he needed to create the enormous federal,
state, and municipal apparatus for making law-and-order politics a
tangible reality.

Looking back at 1968 from our present moment is particularly
poignant given the surging power of the contemporary right and the
enormous obstacles confronting the current movement for Black
lives. There are, however, optimistic lessons to be drawn from 1968 as
well. Foremost, perhaps, is the way that activists responded to injury
by fashioning new forms of oppositional politics and analysis. In the
face of the unwillingness of SNCC's male leadership to address issues
of gender equity, reproductive rights, and the everyday problems of
women in the organization, a group of female members founded the
Black Women's Liberation Committee (BWLC), the direct prede-
cessor to the Third World Women's Alliance. This new organization
interrogated how overlapping systems of race, gender, and imperial
power converged in non-white women's experience. The following
year, one of the BWLC's charter members, Frances Beal, published the

pamphlet *Double Jeopardy*, thereby laying the intellectual groundwork for the articulation of intersectionality in the late 1980s. Similarly, the BPP countered the imprisonment of its cofounder by launching the "Free Huey Movement" in 1968. Responding to the immense scale of repression they faced, the Panthers inverted the terms of engagement by placing the state on trial and propelling the concept of the political prisoner into the American mainstream. Their campaign expanded the ranks of the party while also sheathing it in a multiracial youth movement opposing state violence at home and abroad. Strikingly, the global dimension of struggle informed both modes of analysis, and at its core was young people's hope that a different world could be fashioned in a time of profound crisis.[8]

PART II

STATE VIOLENCE
AND THE WAR(S) ON CRIME

CHAPTER 3

WHO'S TO BLAME
FOR MASS INCARCERATION?

The images inspired by Michael Javen Fortner's new book, *Black Silent Majority*, are revealing. A *New Yorker* review featured a graphic rendering of somber Black men clad in orange jumpsuits imprisoned behind a fence made from the bodies of neatly dressed Black men and women.[1] Strikingly, the impediments are faceless, with only an occasional wisp of pink lip or sculpted facial hair, but the period-piece A-line skirts, peg leg suits, and skinny ties speak for themselves. The respectable classes of Fortner's "Black silent majority" form a literal wall of Black human bondage. Through the magic of design, the book's thesis is rendered in a deeply visceral way: African Americans themselves, not white backlash against Black advancement, mobilized the phalanx behind mass incarceration.

• • •

Black Silent Majority is an ambitious and provocative book by a young African American political scientist, who argues that "working- and middle-class African Americans are partially responsible for the mass incarceration of Black sons, brothers, husbands, and fathers and the misery that they endured while committed to penal institutions in

---

* "Who's to Blame for Mass Incarceration?" originally appeared in *Boston Review* (2015). Reprinted with permission.

New York." Fortner takes aim at a whole body of scholarship, journal-
istic writings, and activist wisdom stressing the centrality of anti-Black
racism to the War on Drugs and, by implication, mass incarceration.
He directs particular ire at Michelle Alexander's bestseller, *The New
Jim Crow* (2010), which forcefully demonstrates how the drug war
and the criminal justice system more broadly have become the biggest obstacle to Black equality since legalized segregation.[2]

One in three African American men will serve time in prison if
present rates persist, leading Alexander to characterize mass incarceration as the most important contemporary form of "racialized social
control." Like the counterrevolution that overthrew Radical Reconstruction and established legalized segregation and convict leasing,
mass incarceration's origins lie, she argues, in the backlash against the
successes of the modern Black freedom struggle: "Mass incarceration—not attacks on affirmative action or lax Civil Rights enforcement—is the most damaging manifestation of the backlash against
the Civil Rights Movement." Alexander's interpretation is far from
unique, reflecting a broad range of new scholarship that understands
race and racism as essential to the punitive turn in American politics
in the years after the Voting Rights Act.[3]

In response, Fortner accuses Alexander and others of oversim-
plifying the origins of the modern carceral state by focusing on white
backlash instead of Black crime victims. "Despite the popularity of
such theories," Fortner argues, "they mask more than they expose. . . .
Crime victims are rendered invisible." This scholarship is guilty of "ig-
noring Black agony." He sets about reclaiming the "agency" of "work-
ing- and middle-class African Americans" suffering at the hands of
"junkies" and a pervasive "Black underclass" sprouted from the urban
decay of the 1960s and '70s.[4]

On Fortner's telling, the supposed Black silent majority countered a tide of intraracial violence with a successful movement against
drugs and crime, culminating in the passage of the Rockefeller Drug

Laws and the takeoff of mass incarceration. Thus Black people themselves, rather than the rightward drift of American politics, are responsible for the huge numbers of Africans Americans languishing in prison. "Mass incarceration had less to do with the white resistance to racial equality and more to do with the Black silent majority's confrontation with the 'reign of criminal terror' in their neighborhoods," he asserts.[5]

Central to Fortner's revisionist project is his desire "to tell it like it is." The choice of Black vernacular signifies his claim to an authentic Black voice as well as his willingness to say unpopular things in service of a larger truth. *Black Silent Majority* opens with a very personal recollection of his traumatic childhood in Brownsville, Brooklyn, punctuated by sirens and gunshots at the height of the 1980s crack crisis. As a toddler, Fortner lost his brother to a stabbing, "the pain and sorrow" of which "stayed in [his] home like accumulated dust."[6] Reading Fortner, one sometimes has the feeling of passing through the racial looking glass and arriving in a strange world where the unlikely pairing of Richard Nixon and Daniel Patrick Moynihan is used to restore historical agency to African Americans. Fortner does not shy away from the words "ghetto," "social pathology," and "Indigenous values," nor do they appear in the distancing embrace of quotation marks. Elsewhere, he casually references Charles Murray's *Losing Ground* (1984) to provide Black-on-Black crime statistics. In many respects, *Black Silent Majority* harkens back to an era of social science innocent of charges of racial bias and prurient representations of African American deviance.[7]

Indeed, Fortner's appropriation of the term "silent majority" is loaded and politicized. The phrase was, after all, central to the Republican rhetoric that mobilized a socially conservative electorate against "Beatniks, taxes, riots, and crime," in Ronald Reagan's words. Coined by Richard Nixon in 1969, the term "silent majority" referred to the nameless, faceless white voters alienated by radical protest, opposition to the Vietnam War, and, perhaps most importantly, the full incorporation of African Americans into the Democratic Party. Over time, the phrase came to signify angry white Republican voters, especially those drawn from the suburban periphery and the American South. Disillusioned by racial liberalism, this disgruntled group abandoned the "mommy party" in search of a politics of law and order and restored national pride. In essence, it was the political and electoral expression of white flight.[8]

Black Silent Majority sets out to prove that, surprisingly, African Americans led this political shift toward punitive crime and drug policy. According to Fortner, one of the most virulent expressions of anti-liberalism arose from the class conflict inside America's postwar "Black ghettos." He sketches an "Indigenous Black morality," distinct from the law-and-order campaigns of the Nixon administration, that responded to a violent crime wave in their segregated neighborhoods. A handful of Black ministers, civic leaders, and ordinary people rallied in support of draconian penalties for drug crimes. Through the "media attention and the activism" generated by this energetic group of Harlemites, New York politicians were "forced" to reckon with the new punitive agenda Black activists were pushing.[9] Fortner explains:

> The Black silent majority supported the regulation and removal of the poor, whom they blamed for urban blight and violence in the streets. After tilting the discursive terrain in the direction of racial equality during the struggles of the civil rights movement, working- and middle-class African Americans tilted it in favor of punitive crime policies and against economic justice for the Black urban poor. As a result, the Black silent majority created an opportunity for the ambitious governor to achieve his own goals and laid the groundwork for mass incarceration.[10]

There is only one problem: no electoral basis exists for this expansive claim, which hinges on a phrase signifying race-based party realignment. In fact, the majority of New York's Black politicians did not support the Rockefeller Drug Laws, nor did their constituents abandon the Democrats for the party of law and order. It is clear from a memo Moynihan sent Nixon in 1970—which includes the term "silent Black majority"—that the president's advisors *hoped* to cultivate a religious and politically and socially conservative segment of the African American community, but Fortner provides no definitive evidence that a Black silent majority existed in reality, as opposed to political rhetoric.

Faced with the inconvenient truth that the overwhelming majority of Black elected officials opposed the Rockefeller Drug Laws—which he doesn't discuss explicitly—Fortner offers tenuous suppositions that lead him into ever-murkier historical waters. The first is his assertion that Black politicians, in the years immediately after the passage of the Voting Rights Act, did not represent the true sentiments of their constituents. "African American elected officials had become more liberal than their constituents because of a generational shift in Black politics," he writes. "In 1973 a large portion of the Black and Puerto Rican Caucus were relatively new members of the legislature and were anchored in the radical politics of the 1960s rather than in traditional Black civil society."[11]

From a writer foregrounding Black agency, the dismissal of this pioneering generation of African American elected officials is somewhat disorienting. After all, the late 1960s and early 1970s witnessed the high tide of the Black Power movement, which found direct expression in electoral politics as the first significant cohort of Black politicians entered municipal, state, and federal politics since Radical Reconstruction. Their assumption of office was made possible by a long, hard struggle against disfranchisement in the South and gerrymandering of Black voter districts in the North. Even more disturbing is Fortner's erasure of key figures from Harlem's homegrown intelligentsia, which suggests that working- and middle-class Blacks had more in common with disgruntled white voters. Thus he makes brash statements about Harlem's political culture in the postwar years, most egregiously dismissing Malcolm X as a figure "not favored by large swaths of New York City's Black community."[12]

So if both African American elected officials and Malcolm X, a former drug user and prisoner memorialized by Ossie Davis as "our own Black shining Prince," are rendered largely irrelevant to the political culture of Black New York in the 1960s, who is integral? The lynchpin of *Black Silent Majority* is a little-known character in Harlem history, Reverend Oberia D. Dempsey, pastor of the Upper Park Avenue Baptist Church and longtime anti-vice crusader. He and a handful of other conservative ministers in Harlem, including Baptist clergymen George W. McMurray and Reverend Earl B. Moore, appeared in a press conference with Nelson A. Rockefeller in January of 1973 to express support for the governor's new drug laws. Dempsey, a former youth minister at Abyssinian Baptist Church and confidant of Rockefeller's, had been an anticrime activist since the early 1960s. Fortner argues somewhat convincingly that Dempsey represented a sector of Black elites and civil advocates, especially those drawn from the ranks of conservative clergy and the National Association for the Advancement of Colored People (NAACP), who emphasized the horrors of crime.

The problem comes when Fortner tries to make Dempsey represent much more: an allegedly monolithic, socially conservative working- and middle-class that he also refers to as "Harlem's moral majority." Curiously, Fortner never lays out with empirical precision who this class of people is and what economic parameters define it. Instead, this so-called Black silent majority emerges in contrast to a pervasive Black underclass whose "reign of criminal terror" (in the NAACP's words) traumatized ordinary citizens. Again, this choice is a profoundly political one. A generation of scholars has debunked the very existence of a Black underclass and shown it to be, much like the crack baby, an ideological fiction that rationalized the Reagan- and Bush-era agenda of welfare reform and mass incarceration.

But Fortner uses this term innocently, as if he were talking about a quantifiable group with uncontested boundaries.

• • •

Historians, including Khalil Gibran Muhammad and Heather Ann Thompson from the National Research Council's Committee on Law and Justice, have raised serious questions about Fortner's use of sources and the overreach of his conclusions. Electoral results undermine Fortner's thesis, so he focuses on the amorphous realms of cultural politics and "traditional Black civil society" reflected in public transcripts from a handful of Black ministers, selective coverage from local newspapers, theatrical productions, media polling data on crime, a handful of primary source documents from the NAACP, and the early journalism of William Raspberry. His use of newspapers is particularly troublesome because, as anyone who writes about crime knows, "what bleeds leads." Newspapers have a vested interest in reporting sensationalized crime stories, and the press has often been a central instigator of moral panics, from the mythical "Negro cocaine fiend" of 1914 to the Reagan-era "crack epidemic."[13]

Equally problematic is Fortner's use of the *Amsterdam News* as a window onto the thoughts and opinions of everyday people. At best, that Harlem newspaper provides a glimpse of how Manhattan's Black elites viewed a particular era. If Fortner had narrowed his conclusions to focus on the privileged segment of Black mandarins represented by the *Amsterdam News*, Raspberry, portions of the NAACP leadership, and conservative clergy, he would have been on much firmer historical ground. With less sweeping conclusions, his book might have contributed to a better understanding of the class and ideological diversity of America's best-known Black metropolis. But, as it stands, *Black Silent Majority* gives a distorted and idiosyncratic view not only of Harlem, but also of postwar America more generally.

Fortner's penchant for conceptual overreach is nowhere more evident than in his treatment of the history of the Republican Party itself. In the final chapter, he takes on the most difficult challenge to his thesis: the consensus view that the primary cause for Rockefeller's shift toward an ultra-punitive stance on crime and drug policy was the political challenge from the right posed by California governor Ronald Reagan. The aging Rockefeller longed to be president, and by the late 1960s he found himself increasingly marginalized in a Republican Party whose demographic base was shifting toward the Sunbelt. Reagan, a close ally of Barry Goldwater, forged an effective strategy of targeting those "rioters and beatniks" to appeal to resentful white working-class voters. Significantly, when Reagan defeated Democratic California incumbent Governor Pat Brown in 1966, he won the majority of white union households. That victory anticipated his presidential win in 1980 and the emergence of the infamous Reagan Democrat.

Rockefeller recognized these shifting ideological sands in the early seventies. Not to be outdone by Reagan's hard-line stance on welfare, crime, and especially Black Power activism, the ambitious Rockefeller crushed the Attica rebellion and passed the nation's toughest drug laws. Fortner equivocates on this point. Toward the end of the book he acknowledges how important this national calculus was to Rockefeller's transformation, but lest it distract the reader from his singular focus on the Black silent majority as causal agent, he elsewhere dismisses not only the importance of the "general mood of the national electorate," but also that of race in party realignment:

> From the Black silent majority in urban black belts to the white silent majority in the suburban Sunbelt, the politics that defined the punitiveness and timing of the Rockefeller Drug Laws as well as the broader narcotics control regime was rooted in the politics of class rather than the politics of race.[14]

On the far side of the racial looking glass, Rockefeller emerges much like a Pontius Pilate figure, whose sacrificial hand is forced by the angry protestations of working- and middle-class African Americans. While *Black Silent Majority*'s liberties with the historical record are disconcerting, at a more philosophical level, its insistence on interpreting trauma and responses to social crisis simply as resolute calls for punishment may be even more troubling. Though Fortner seeks to resurrect the lived experience of Black people, he is deaf to Harlem residents' demands for more social welfare and state redistribution to alleviate poverty, the primary cause of crime itself. Strikingly, he dismisses as unrepresentative Kenneth Clark, A. Philip Randolph, and Black elected leaders who sought social democratic solutions to the problems of urban divestment, redlining, and institutionalized racism.

Absent from *Black Silent Majority* is an examination of what happens when a marginalized community facing mass capital abandonment, job loss, and an urgent public health crisis is presented only one policy option: more policing and punishment. The book offers no discussion of the Nixon administration's 1971 declaration of a War on Drugs and its establishment three years earlier of the federal Law Enforcement Assistance Administration, which, through funding tough-on-crime measures, provided strong incentives for the punitive turn across the United States. This omission is not accidental. After all, Fortner's thesis hinges on the idea that the vengeful campaign that culminated in the Rockefeller Drug Laws emerged from "Indigenous construction" of an autarchic "Black ghetto" riddled by class conflict and violence.

While Fortner declares his concern for Black crime victims, his book exhibits a distinct lack of empathy not only for drug users but also for the ordinary Harlemites he ostensibly champions. He writes that Harlem "needed urban renewal as much as a cultural renaissance," referring to the sorts of city building projects that tended to demolish poor and minority neighborhoods to make room for new development, highways, and other public works. He speaks of the Black silent majority itself in somewhat contemptuous terms, explaining, for example, how "drug addicts . . . pilfered the symbols of their thin yet meaningful success: television sets, fur coats, and the hubcaps on their Cadillacs." Ultimately, Fortner appears less interested in telling the stories of victimized people than in mobilizing their very existence to justify his claims that African Americans themselves were a driving force behind the drug war and mass incarceration and that an overwhelmingly reactionary Black working- and middle-class repudiated Black militancy and racial liberalism in favor of law and order.

• • •

In numerous popular and scholarly venues, Fortner has accused his critics, many of whom are fellow Black academics, of a political witch-hunt. But this claim elides his book's explicit ideological content. At its core, *Black Silent Majority* takes aim at the antiracist ideas that have inspired much of the youthful protest of the past several years. Implicit in the Ferguson protests, Black Lives Matter, We Charge Genocide, and the panoply of new Black activist organizations that have sprung up since Michael Brown's murder in August 2014 is the understanding not only that mass incarceration and militarized policing are inherently anti-Black, but also that the carceral state itself is an expression of white backlash against African American gains in the post–Civil Rights era.

A curious contradiction lies at the heart of Fortner's book. While he decries the abuses of mass incarceration, if you take the activism of his Black silent majority at face value, then mass incarceration would seem a logical and just outcome. In a recent *New York Times* op-ed, he inches toward precisely this position by valorizing an idea forcefully expressed by former New York mayor Rudolph Giuliani: that African Americans' failure to reckon with Black-on-Black crime calls into question their mobilization against police killings and state-sanctioned violence. Downplaying the expediency of social welfare efforts, Fortner asserts, "Long-term strategies provide little immediate relief from the daily horrors of urban crime. In the short run, we need the police. . . . We can't eliminate the propensity to over-police and over-imprison unless we curb the disorder and chaos that threaten and destroy urban Black lives."[15]

There is no doubt that, within the large and diverse African American population in the United States, anticrime sentiment existed both in the Rockefeller era and now. Indeed, in the Reagan years, the cry for punishment of drug sellers and users was much louder, and unlike in the early 1970s, this stance included a majority of the Congressional Black Caucus. It is hardly surprising that people who were forced to face the problems of poverty, addiction, and economic abandonment expressed anger and looked to the state for solutions. What Fortner misses about the overlapping wars on drugs and crime, though, is that the poorest among us are most likely to experience crime, and that includes low-income drug users, people working off the books, the formerly incarcerated, and other vulnerable populations. But they are not defined as victims, because that status is one of racial and class privilege. *Black Silent Majority* skillfully incorporates and blunts opposing arguments but refuses to take seriously the consequences of poverty, redlining, and other forms of structural exclusion. As harm reduction specialist Gabor Maté has argued, behind every drug crisis lies a tale of social heartbreak. Selectively elevating conservative Black voices that were themselves exploited for the political benefit of others is no way to honor that painful history or to prevent its repetition.[16]

CHAPTER 4

Crack in Los Angeles

Black Response to the Late Twentieth-Century War on Drugs

n the winter of 1985, the Los Angeles Police Department (LAPD) unveiled a signature new weapon in the city's drug war. With Chief Daryl F. Gates copiloting, the Special Weapons and Tactics Team (SWAT) used a fourteen-foot battering ram attached to an "armored vehicle" to break into a house in Pacoima. After tearing a "gaping hole" in one of the outside walls of the house, police found two women and three children inside, eating ice cream. SWAT uncovered negligible quantities of illicit drugs, and the district attorney subsequently declined to prosecute. In the days following the raid, Black clergy and the San Fernando Valley chapter of the National Association for the Advancement of Colored People (NAACP) organized a protest rally in a local church. "We don't need new weapons to be tried out on us," Rev. Jeffrey Joseph exclaimed. "Of all the methods that there are to arrest a person, they used a brand-new toy." Not all members of the African American community agreed, however. City councilman David Cunningham, who represented South Los Angeles, praised Gates's actions. "Go right ahead, Chief. You do whatever you can to get rid of these rock houses. They're going to destroy the Black community if you don't."[1]

---

* "Crack in Los Angeles: Black Response to the Late Twentieth-Century War on Drugs" originally appeared in *Journal of American History* 102, no 1 (2015): 162–73. Reprinted with permission of *Journal of American History*.

These divergent responses embody the core contradiction produced by crack cocaine and the War on Drugs for African American communities of Los Angeles in the 1980s. On the one hand, these locations faced an unprecedented scale in the militarization of policing, arrests, and incarceration, but on the other, many people—drawn especially from the ranks of the middle class—saw crack use, distribution, and intracommunity violence as comparable if not greater threats. To address this sense of urgency, the activist-scholar Clarence Lusane used the term "drug crisis" to differentiate it from the state-sponsored and moral-panic–driven discourse of the "crack epidemic." Lusane's formulation is valuable not only for its discussion of crack's impact on communities of color in Los Angeles but also for assisting historians in excavating how the state mobilized and appropriated a range of reactions—including fear, anger, and disorientation—in African American communities to justify repression and the increased militarization of law enforcement.[2]

Understanding our national drug war requires disentangling the social history of drug use, informal economy, and poverty from law-and-order narratives rationalizing punitive campaigns. In hindsight, it is clear that the state appropriated real anxieties from Black urban areas (such as Harlem and South Los Angeles) that were experiencing rapid economic decline and used these concerns to rationalize its wars on drugs. Not only did this strategy appeal to racial antipathies among white voters, but it also hindered political opposition to the drug war by African Americans who were desperately seeking solutions to the public health and social crises facing their neighborhoods. This dynamic was certainly not unique to New York and Los Angeles. During the Reagan administration, Democrats and Republicans across the country strongly supported the War on Drugs. Given the now-infamous racial impact of sentencing for crack cocaine possession, consumption, and distribution, Black elected officials' near-unanimous support for Ronald Reagan's 1986 Anti-Drug Abuse

Act reveals an important paradox. The progressive California congressman Ronald V. Dellums, along with fifteen other members of
the Congressional Black Caucus, actually cosponsored the bill, which
resulted in the 100-to-1 sentencing disparity for crack versus powder
cocaine in federal drug cases, resulting in the disproportionate incarceration of large numbers of African American offenders.

While significant Black support for the militarized war(s) on
drugs and gangs in the 1980s may seem surprising and counterin-
tuitive, this article reflects on how deeply divisive punishment campaigns proved for African American populations. This conflict was
nowhere more evident than in late twentieth-century Los Angeles—"the world's largest retail market for cocaine" and the epicenter
of the US crack economy. During the 1980s, militarized campaigns
against drugs and gangs resulted in new and brutal technologies of
policing and criminalization focused on South Central Los Angeles.
Despite these high-profile measures, surprisingly little opposition to
these practices appeared initially, even from those who suffered their
worst effects. Black Angelinos divided along lines of class, ideology,
faith, and age in their attempts to address neighborhoods in crisis.
However, by the early 1990s multiple sites of resistance began to
emerge. Starting with the early efforts of the Coalition against Police
Abuse (CAPA) through the work of the Community Coalition for
Substance Abuse Prevention and Treatment, and the work of Mothers Reclaim Our Children, Black residents in ever-larger numbers
challenged hypermilitarized policing and the large-scale prison warehousing of youth of color.[3]

MILITARIZATION OF POLICING AND THE WAR ON DRUGS

Heather Ann Thompson has argued that the history of mass incarceration remains largely unwritten, and this is nowhere truer than
in the history of the US war(s) on drugs. Despite growing visibility

via public denunciations and proclamations of failure, the history of America's drug wars is largely unknown. This is surprising given the wars' catalytic role in one of the largest state-building enterprises of the late twentieth century: mass incarceration. Scholars have documented that between 1985 and 2000, drug offenses were two-thirds of the increase in federal inmates and half of the increase in state prison populations.[4]

In 1971 President Richard M. Nixon coined the phrase War on Drugs, but in reality, the undertaking was neither a single coherent entity nor a true war, but rather a succession of executive-sponsored domestic and transnational punitive campaigns spanning the postwar era through today. The declaration of war mandated increased resources to fight the "drug crisis" while also initiating a conflict without end. The criminologist Jerome H. Skolnick used the term "semi-martial state" to describe the effect of the drug war on the nation. At the federal, state, and local levels, such a punitive turn in government resulted in the criminalization of large segments of the US population for illicit drug consumption, possession, and distribution. Although Skolnick's analysis focused on the proposed multibillion-dollar increase for federal enforcement and interdiction in 1989, during the decade preceding the appointment of William Bennett as "drug czar," Los Angeles exemplified how the drug war intensified the militarization of domestic policing. The city's multiple overlapping wars against drugs, gangs, and crime reflected Skolnick's semi-martial state in terms of fiscal expenditures and institutional practices of law enforcement, prisons, courts, and parole.[5]

Punitive campaigns against drugs and gangs in Los Angeles rationalized a new martial infrastructure. The state applied militarization unequally by focusing on historic African American and Latino neighborhoods in the South Central part of the city. As in counterinsurgency strategy, the geographic application of force meant that particular populations were at high risk not only because of their age and race but also because of their location. Indeed, by 1992 city sheriffs listed nearly half of the African American men under age twenty-five in Los Angeles County as gang members. The ultimate carceral effects of this mass criminalization can hardly be overstated. The California Department of Corrections (CDC) prison population increased from 19,623 in 1977 to 162,000 in the year 2000 with over 40 percent drawn from Los Angeles and 70 percent from Southern California. By 1990 drug offenses were 34.2 percent of new admissions to California prisons and 25 percent of detainees in the Los Angeles County Jail, which contained the world's largest urban prison population. The carceral effects were not, however, equally distributed. Numerous studies show the extreme racial disparities of mass incarceration and the War on Drugs, and California arguably led this national trend. By the year 2000 the combined numbers of Blacks and Latinos were over 64 percent of the total population of the CDC. Furthermore, African Americans were roughly 7 percent of California's general population but accounted for 31 percent of the state's prisoners.[6]

Major components of the militarized infrastructure of the LAPD, the Los Angeles Sheriff's Department (LASD), and the California Highway Patrol could be traced to law enforcement's hostile response to the civil unrest of the postwar years. In the aftermath of the 1965 Watts rebellions, the LAPD's use of military-grade hardware and elite tactical units originated in the department's counterinsurgency campaigns against the Black Power and Brown Power movements. Under the leadership of Chief William Parker (from 1950 to 1966), Chief Tom Reddin (from 1967 to 1969), and Chief Edward M. Davis (from 1969 to 1978), the LAPD developed signature policing strategies that became essential to the city's brutal prosecution of the wars on drugs and gangs two decades later. The department founded SWAT with a compact force of former military veterans in 1967. Subsequently, the LAPD deployed SWAT for the first time against the Southern California Black Panther party's office. The commando force used a tank on loan from the California National Guard and won US Department of Justice authorization for a grenade launcher.[7]

SWAT marked a new era in Los Angeles law enforcement, defined by the steady expansion of the use of elite tactical units at the expense of rank-and-file patrol officers. With funding from the Law Enforcement Assistance Administration, the department created Total Resources Against Southeast Hoodlums (TRASH) five years later. Responding to community protest, the name was changed to Community Resources Against Street Hoodlums (CRASH), and the organization went on to become the city's most notorious antigang unit in the 1980s, with the LASD's program Operation Safe Streets and the district attorney's Hardcore Drug Unit following in its wake. As this list of martial alphabet agencies implies, starting with the invention of SWAT, Los Angeles led the national militarization of policing—a subject yet to be comprehensively addressed by historians. One of the most urgent tasks is to document local law enforcement's nationwide effort to acquire weaponry during the earlier era of mass protest and to trace how this changed over time, particularly in the post–Cold War period of military surplus and during the counterterrorism push following the September 11, 2001, attacks.[8]

Another striking feature of departmental militarization, in addition to personnel restructuring that funneled more manpower and funding toward elite commando units, was the LAPD's attempt to expunge all social service components from policing and to focus exclusively on crime and territorial control. Geographic dispersion of the city and the establishment of the LAPD Air Support Division in 1974—which became the largest "airborne municipal law enforcement system in the world"—contributed to tactical surveillance of and distance from city residents. While Chief Parker's vision of professionalization in the postwar years laid the foundation for this approach, under the auspices of the Reagan era's intensified wars on crime, drugs, and gangs, the martial imperative grew stronger and received large increases in funding (especially through expanding asset forfeiture) and direct support from municipal, state, and federal governments. According to the Los Angeles American Civil Liberties Union, "the political rhetoric about a 'war' on drugs and a 'war' on crime ... helped turn the police into soldiers—not civil servants or guardians of the community order—making them sometimes more aggressive and forceful than they have a right to be in pursuit of criminals and suspects."[9]

Los Angeles's high-profile War on Drugs reflected the larger policies and strategic aims of Reagan's national punishment campaign, including saturation policing, eradication of youth gangs, asset forfeiture, federalization of drug charges, and strict enforcement of mandatory minimum sentencing. At the street level, use of massive police sweeps with spectacular displays of overwhelming force embodied the city's militarized vision of law enforcement, as did Chief Gates's repeated calls to arms. Testifying on the one-year anniversary of the George H. W. Bush administration's War on Drugs, the LAPD chief told the Senate Judiciary Committee that "the casual drug user ought to be taken out and shot." Behind his bombastic rhetoric lay a larger truth. In an era of deindustrialization and drastic reductions in social services, mass incarceration fueled by antidrug and antigang campaigns became de facto urban social policy for the residents of impoverished communities such as South Central Los Angeles and Pico Union. The prescription for widespread joblessness and the illicit economies that accompanied urban divestment was simply to remove a significant percentage of the population from the streets through prison warehousing. Tellingly, in 1980—prior to the advent of the alleged "crack epidemic" and Reagan's declaration of a new War on Drugs—Gates argued that the 0.1 percent incarceration rate for California's population (26,000 people) was insufficient. To achieve greater public safety, he advocated that between 2 and 3 percent of California's residents should be locked up.[10]

One of the major challenges for understanding the municipal and national histories of the US war(s) on drugs is tracing their symbiosis with and prosecution through related punitive campaigns against gangs, crime, and—in later years—terrorism. In Los Angeles, for example, much of the carceral infrastructure for the city's War on Drugs relied on geographically targeted gang sweeps combined with antigang legislation and prosecution tools. Moreover, the conflation of drug crimes with street gang membership created a comprehensive net for the criminalization of nonwhite youth. The LAPD's selective arrest and prosecution of youth of color meant that the category of "gang" became inherently racialized. Drawing on a repertoire of historical "demonologies" with specific prosecutorial regimes, the LAPD alternately viewed Black and Latino gangs through the lens of organized crime or terrorism. "It's probably a misnomer to call them street gangs," argued an LAPD lieutenant member of CRASH. "What we are seeing is the first indication of Black organized crime." Far from unique, the slippage from street gangs to drug trafficking, organized crime, and terrorism represented the defining principle of the Reagan-Bush era War on Drugs. Its solution was total suppression and use of Racketeer Influenced and Corrupt Organizations Act prosecutions to remove as many alleged gang members from the streets as possible. Between 1984 and 1988 California passed over eighty separate antigang measures and developed powerful new legal tools, including the civil gang injunction and gang enhancements in sentencing. In December 1987, the Los Angeles city attorney and future mayor James Hahn pioneered the injunction's use against the Playboy Gangster Crips from West Los Angeles. Gang injunctions permanently prohibited members from engaging in specified behaviors in a designated geographic area. The prosecuting agency sued a gang as an "unincorporated association," to allow for the addition of new names to prosecutorial lists. The injunction's civil nature also meant that the state was not required to provide a public defender.[11]

Defining the War on Drugs as a war on gangs justified the criminalization of everyday life in Black and Brown Los Angeles. Modes
of dress, movement, color of shoelaces, hand gestures, and mere
association became defined as prosecutable offenses. Gang injunctions worked in tandem with municipal, state, and federal databases.
In 1985 the LASD created a computerized list, the Gang Reporting
Evaluation and Tracking system (GREAT). Seven years later, the federal government's General Accounting Office revealed that the city's
sheriffs listed 47 percent of all African American men in Los Angeles County between the ages of twenty-one and twenty-four as gang
members. Racially targeted policing combined with the denial of legal representation made it virtually impossible for youth to have their
names removed from GREAT. In this sense antigang injunctions also
contained a brutal class component: their success hinged on their targets' inability to hire lawyers.[12]

While antigang injunctions and databases provided mechanisms
for surveillance, control, and the assumption of large numbers of minority youth into "the system" for minor offenses, gang enhancement
legislation ultimately aided the process of mass incarceration. In 1988
the California legislature passed the Street Terrorism Enforcement
and Prevention (STEP) Act, which mandated that convicted persons
who have been designated as gang members face additional charges
and sentencing. In the initial 1988 law, prosecutors could "enhance"
gang members' convictions with one to five years of additional time
in state prison per offense. Subsequently, California's Proposition 21
amended the STEP Act in 2000 by increasing gang enhancements to
sixteen months to five years for nonviolent offenses and to ten, fifteen,
twenty, and twenty-five years to life for violent offenses. Moreover, in
first-degree murder cases with special circumstances, Proposition 21
mandated the death penalty or life imprisonment without the possibility of parole. The dense layering of the STEP Act and its subsequent
revisions, including added prison time for gun charges and for crimes

committed within one thousand yards of a school, meant that it was not uncommon for very young offenders to receive multiple consecutive life sentences.[13]

Los Angeles's repressive legal regime worked in tandem with law enforcement's spectacular shows of force, mass arrests, and saturation policing. After the 1988 murder of the suburban teenager Karen Toshima, the LAPD proclaimed 1988 the "year of the gang enforcement." "This is war," declared Chief Gates. "We want to get the message out to the cowards out there . . . that we're going to come and get them." With this battle cry, the department sent over one thousand officers into South Los Angeles in conjunction with Operation Hammer. On April 9, 1988, the police set up an impromptu holding facility in the parking lot of the Los Angeles Coliseum and proceeded to arrest over 1,400 people—including more African American youth than in any other single incident since the Watts rebellions twenty-three years earlier. Over the course of the next six months, law enforcement jailed over eighteen thousand people, declaring over half of the arrests as "gang related." The price in human and financial terms was considerable; journalists estimated that Operation Hammer cost up to $150,000 per day. Significantly, the prosecutors charged only a handful of people with actual crimes.[14]

THE CRACK CRISIS AND BLACK RESPONSE TO THE WAR ON DRUGS

Historians have yet to write the top-down institutional history of municipal, state, and federal antidrug and antigang campaigns since the Reagan era, but even more neglected are broad questions about framing that link the crack crisis to the militarization of the drug wars. Integral to this silence is the lack of research into how communities of color responded to this punishment regime across region and time. Social scientists have debated Black support for Nixon-era law-and-order campaigns; however, historians have yet to explore how African American and Latino populations across the country understood, experienced, and reacted to the war(s) on drugs and gangs in the era of mass incarceration since the late 1970s. The history of Black Los Angeles offers some compelling insights into this largely uncharted territory and raises a number of issues that warrant further study and exploration. The first is the conceptual question of framing. During the 1980s much of the discourse from Black politicians and the press centered on the crack crisis rather than on the repressive apparatus of the war(s) on drugs and gangs. In Los Angeles, at the epicenter of crack use and distribution, the scale of panic can hardly be overestimated. In 1989 California representative Maxine Waters declared, "The most urgent problem facing ghettoized African Americans today is the lethal infestation of drugs in our communities." Although the solutions that Waters sought emphasized social welfare and public health for troubled neighborhoods reeling from Reagan-era divestment, the lens of crisis unwittingly strengthened law enforcement's justification for the semi-martial state of the drug war and provided it with a thin humanitarian veil.[15]

In many respects, the timing of the drug war in Los Angeles could not have been worse. For years, the local African American community had been fighting to rein in the LAPD. On the eve of Reagan's War on Drugs, the Coalition Against Police Abuse scored a decisive victory against the LAPD in 1978, leading to the dissolution of the department's Public Disorder Intelligence Division. The former Black Panther Michael Zinzun had founded CAPA in 1976, and it became one of the most sustained grassroots efforts to stop police violence in Los Angeles. Tragically, just as the courts mandated that the LAPD implement these reforms, the state launched a new phase in the War on Drugs. The professed exigencies of this militarized campaign reversed many activists' earlier gains while simultaneously narrowing the horizon of public debate to punishment-based solutions.[16]

The moral panic over crack, like the concern about PCP (Phencyclidine, known popularly in Los Angeles as "Sherm") in years prior, obscured the militarization of law enforcement and its geopolitical context. One difficult task for historians is to disaggregate the genuine concerns and problems of African American neighborhoods during this period from state and mainstream media portrayals of the "crack epidemic." The Reagan administration invoked African American suffering—with the "crack baby" as its most potent trope—to rationalize a new and vastly intensified carceral regime. Too often, state- and media-driven narratives of the Reagan era have saturated the popular imagination while, in fact, the social history of Black urban communities in the 1980s and 1990s remains largely undocumented. In contrast to sensationalized portrayals, the themes of social service retrenchment, deindustrialization, intensification of poverty, and structural isolation are as foundational to the period as drug consumption, illicit economies, and the restructuring of the traditional nuclear family. Demystifying the racial myths of the crack era also requires careful, nuanced exploration of the complex interplay of race and class because African American politicians and elite service providers also participated in the drug war's pervasive rhetoric of crisis.[17]

Black class politics in the post–Civil Rights era proved integral to community approaches to the drug wars. Historically, Black Angelinos had the largest intraracial income gap nationally, and economic disparity shaped how different strata understood the War on Drugs. In the early 1980s white-led middle-class reformist organizations sponsored popular marches calling attention to the plight of neighborhoods in South Central Los Angeles and East Los Angeles. In July 1985, shortly after the ACLU won an injunction against the use of the LAPD's battering ram, nearly ten thousand residents gathered on the downtown campus of St. Mary's College for an anticrime rally. The Southern California Organizing Committee (SCOC) and the United

Neighborhoods Organization (UNO) of East Los Angeles cospon-sored the protest. Formed in 1982 by a network of churches, SCOC mixed law-and-order politics with maternalistic advocacy for social welfare and youth programs. Given historical fights for adequate po-licing and higher rates of violent crime in South Los Angeles—Af-rican Americans were six times more likely than whites to be killed by homicide—their concerns were not surprising. Nevertheless, the hallmarks of militarized law enforcement remained unmistakable in the organizations' punitive visions of reform. SCOC and UNO ad-vocated establishing "combat zone" teams drawn from multiple law enforcement agencies to target "gangs" and "drug traffickers" in high-crime areas; higher taxes on liquor to pay for more police; increases in federal drug agents in Los Angeles; and, perhaps most importantly, building a Black and Brown coalition to force local officials to pro-vide more police protection. "We come here to make a choice today," argued Father Luis Olivares of La Placita Church. "We can fight those who stuff drugs into our children, or we can just sit on our butts and wish that it weren't so."[18]

As this rhetoric shows, the crack crisis proved deeply divisive and helped fracture African American and Latino communities internally along lines of age, class, and faith. In the context of massive cuts to American cities under the Reagan administration, carceral solutions to problems of impoverished communities had much greater efficacy than redistributive liberalism. Rather than approaching the problem via public health or structural inequality (deindustrialization, out-sourcing, capital flight), these early reformers looked to the problems and contradictions inside impoverished neighborhoods. Christian churches, in particular, played an important role in advocating for more punitive, self-help approaches. How welfare retrenchment and militarized law enforcement with its crisis-driven rationale fostered an increasingly conservative grassroots "politics of personal respon-sibility" is an understudied theme in the history of Los Angeles and throughout Black America in the era of mass incarceration and the war(s) on drugs. Paradoxically, while some of the residents of South Los Angeles initially supported the drug wars in hopes of protecting their children from the perceived scourge of crack, it soon became apparent that these very youth were being subjected to militarized police sweeps, gang injunctions and enhancements, and mandatory sentencing laws. For many, the punishment infrastructure driving mass incarceration proved more destructive than the original problems of drug addiction, use, and sale.

The state effectively co-opted much of the anger and disorientation created by the Reagan-era urban crisis into an anticrime framework that blamed the pathological culture of Black and Brown youth for the problems of poverty and urban divestment. Los Angeles's sharp intraracial class divide exacerbated this tendency to target the poorest and most vulnerable members of the community. Therefore, elected officials, the clergy, and traditional Civil Rights leadership cannot be used as the sine qua non of Black popular opinion. Indeed, writing about the wars on drugs and gangs in the late twentieth century provides a window into Black class polarities and antagonisms in the post–Civil Rights era. Sectors of Black elites—from the administration of Los Angeles mayor Tom Bradley to SCOC—supported Los Angeles's War on Drugs and gangs, but the responses of the majority of low-income residents in South Los Angeles remain harder to discern through traditional historical sources. More social research into how the intraracial factors of class, homeownership, and neighborhood geography affected law-and-order attitudes within communities of color is desperately needed. For scholars attempting to recover this history, the techniques of ethnography and oral history are essential. Too often, African American elites, who by definition have left stronger archival traces, have been treated as representative of the Black community as a whole. The history of the Coalition Against Police Abuse offers an intriguing example of how we might differentiate Black poor and working-class "drug war politics" from the politics of their wealthier counterparts.

In the early 1990s a palpable shift took place as a variety of African American–led organizations proposed alternate frameworks to the semi-martial state of the Los Angeles drug and gang wars. The cumulative effects of mass criminalization, mandatory minimum sentencing, disparate crack prosecution, and the expansive municipal, state, and federal apparatus created to criminalize drug use, distribution, and alleged gang participation resulted in an explosion of the population in jails and prisons. As residents watched this expansion, a commitment to developing less punitive approaches emerged. Redefining the crack crisis in terms of public health, structural economic decline, and as a product of Reagan-era anticommunist foreign policy was a powerful tool for mobilizing anti–drug war sentiment in the African American community of Los Angeles. This shift took place, however, within the confines of fiscal and political restraints. As historians document resistance to the carceral state and the War on Drugs, exploring how social service retrenchment, neoliberal restructuring, and pro-market governance influenced African American and Latino modes of protest is crucial background. In contrast to the era of the Great Society and the long Black freedom movement, by the early 1990s not-for-profit organizations and community development corporations competed with grassroots social movements as the legitimate medium for organized dissent.[19]

In 1990, future California representative Karen Bass sponsored an inaugural conference, "Crack: Crisis in the African American Community," to help launch the Community Coalition for Substance Abuse Prevention and Treatment. The new organization countered the rationale for militarized law enforcement by redefining crack addiction more broadly as a public "health crisis." Having worked as a physician's assistant at the Los Angeles County–University of Southern California Medical Center emergency room, Bass had witnessed the devastating effects of addiction. "I just really became obsessed with how the drug problem, specifically the crack epidemic, was impacting the community," she later explained. The Community Coalition advocated mandatory school counseling, drug and gang diversion programs, and utilizing "forfeiture-seizure" monies to finance drug treatment. "Our mission, essentially, is to address the drug and alcohol problems of the community," Bass explained. "We don't do that by providing direct services such as treatment or counseling, but we do that by organizing and empowering community residents to change the environment that creates drug and alcohol problems in the first place." The Community Coalition's most sustained activism centered on preventing liquor stores from reopening after the 1992 Los Angeles rebellions. Modeling its efforts on homeowner associations, the coalition organized residents to clean up the streets. By eliminating the environment that fostered crime and addiction, including liquor stores, transient hotels, and open-air sex and drug markets, the coalition sought to transform the "hopelessness and despair" of South Central Los Angeles.[20]

In the penumbra of Los Angeles's 1992 rebellions, other Black voices emerged, directly critiquing state violence, police militarization, and US foreign policy. Foremost among these was CAPA, with roots predating the Reagan era and stretching deep into the Los Angeles Black Power movement. At the height of the city's militarized War on Drugs, CAPA's small cadre of activists taught community members how to document police abuses, utilize media, and wage legal campaigns. Michael Zinzun's successful lawsuits against the LAPD and the Pasadena police and his critique of state violence and mass incarceration, combined with his nurturance of younger activists, helped forge an intergenerational channel for radical activism. CAPA's motto, "We will work with you not for you," reflected its preference for egalitarian, decentralized modes of organizing. Nevertheless, during the 1980s the group struggled to attract a broader base and often found itself overshadowed by more mainstream, punitive efforts. In the early 1990s, however, CAPA gained greater visibility as the carceral effects of a decade-long war on Black and Brown youth became visible in the vast increase in the incarceration of youth of color. From 1982 to 1995 the numbers of African Americans in the California Department of Corrections increased from 12,470 to 42,296, while Latino incarceration grew from 9,006 to 46,080.[21]

Together with Mothers Reclaim Our Children and the California Gang Truce, CAPA and its network of grassroots radicals embodied a foundational historical shift as poor and working-class populations of color who suffered the worst effects of Los Angeles's militarized drug wars began mobilizing against gang suppression and mass incarceration. Far to the left of Black elected officials, the local clergy, and traditional Civil Rights activists, these new political formations raise a number of compelling issues for future scholarship on the War on Drugs. The first is the need for more social history of poor and working-class "drug war politics," ranging from formal organizations in cities across the United States to everyday infrapolitics of resistance. Second, scholars must carefully parse the chronology and periodization of Black and Brown opposition to the carceral state. As is clear in the history of Los Angeles's militarized wars on drugs and gangs, a significant shift occurred over a two-decade period, and this same attention to change over time must inform research on punishment campaigns from the initial passage of the Rockefeller Drug Laws in 1973 through today.[22]

When viewed in hindsight, the racial intent and effects of the late twentieth-century wars on drugs and gangs in Los Angeles are very clear. By 1995, after thirteen years of the Reagan-Bush War on Drugs, California incarcerated African Americans at rates nearly five times their percentage of the general population. The extreme militarization of policing focused on the criminalization, control, and prison warehousing of an entire generation of Black and Brown youth. Los Angeles's development of the first SWAT in the nation anticipated and arguably led the martial turn a decade before the rise of mass incarceration rates. During the Reagan era, however, the new powers, funding, and ideological mandate bestowed on police and prosecutors vastly intensified warfare on drugs and gangs in which the line between the police and the military became more permeable. Yet many within the African American community in Los Angeles and elsewhere initially found mobilizing against this semi-martial regime difficult. Black residents, and homeowners in particular, understood the crisis within their own neighborhoods of spiraling poverty, crack use and sale, and intraracial violence as equally perilous. The extreme polarization of wealth among Black Angelinos exacerbated this tendency and created fault lines of social class and incarceration status. While the LAPD, SWAT, CRASH, and Operation Safe Streets besieged neighborhoods such as South Central, Watts, and Pico-Union, wealthy enclaves such as Baldwin and Windsor Hills remained largely insulated from domestic warfare against the poor and most vulnerable.[23]

Los Angeles was certainly not unique. Many Black politicians and other prominent leaders supported drastic carceral policies in hopes of staunching the crack crisis facing Black communities across the country. While Councilman David Cunningham's support for Chief Gates's use of the battering ram represented the far-right wing of Los Angeles's African American elected officials, Rep. Charles Rangel of New York emerged as a vocal antidrug warrior and advocate for the expansion of police and prosecutorial powers. However, in Los Angeles this dynamic changed significantly as the carceral effects of the race to punishment became fully visible. A new generation of organizers, nurtured by longtime activists such as Michael Zinzun, centered in the communities of Watts and South Central Los Angeles, redefined the solutions to neighborhoods in crisis. The formerly incarcerated and their families, gang members, veteran organizers, and other vulnerable segments of the population caught in the crosshairs of the militarized drug war articulated a new form of poor and working-class "drug war politics" that emphasized structural police violence, the development of grassroots, Indigenous solutions rather than state punishment, and the role of US foreign policy in creating the crack crisis. As the first generation of carceral state historiography is written, Los Angeles's War on Drugs is instructive. The city embodied many of the war's worst aspects, and despite this history—or perhaps because of it—produced some of its most compelling opposition.

CHAPTER 5

The Clintons' War on Drugs

When Black Lives Didn't Matter

In August 2015, an uncomfortable encounter between Black Lives Matter activists and Hillary Clinton finally broke the silence of many mainstream press outlets on the Clintons' shared responsibility for the disastrous policies of mass incarceration and its catalyst, the War on Drugs. Although a number of prominent academics have written on the subject, little popular discussion of the racial impact of the Clintons' crime and punishment policies emerged until the opening volleys of the 2016 presidential race.[1]

A grainy cell-phone video of the incident showed a handful of young (BLMM/M4BL) protestors confronting Hillary Clinton on the campaign trail in New Hampshire. After expressing her ardent feminism and pride in meeting a female presidential candidate, Daunasia Yancey forcefully confronted Clinton about her shared culpability in America's destructive War on Drugs: "You and your family have been personally and politically responsible for policies that have caused health and human services disasters in impoverished communities of color through the domestic and international War on Drugs that you championed as first lady, senator, and secretary of state." Yancey continued, "And so I just want to know how you feel

---

* "The Clintons' War on Drugs: When Black Lives Didn't Matter" originally appeared in *False Choices: The Faux Feminism of Hillary Rodham Clinton* (Verso Books, 2016). Reprinted with permission.

about your role in that violence, and how you plan to reverse it?"[2]

Yancey's question deftly turned Hillary's use of her husband's presidency as political qualification on its head: if her term as first lady deeply involved in policy issues qualifies her for the presidency, then she could be held responsible for policies made during those years. The Clintons had used the concept of personal responsibility to shame poor Blacks for their economic predicament. Indeed, Bill Clinton titled his notorious welfare-to-work legislation "The Personal Responsibility and Work Opportunity Reconciliation Act of 1996." Yancey's question forced the Democratic front-runner to accept personal responsibility for mass incarceration policies passed under Bill Clinton's administration.

Hillary Clinton's response to the activists was telling. She attributed the policies of mass incarceration and the War on Drugs to "the very real concerns" of communities of color and poor people, who faced a crime wave in the 1980s and 1990s. Echoing an argument that is gaining greater purchase in certain elite circles as the movement against racialized state violence and incarceration sweeps across the US, Clinton deflected the charge of anti-Black animus back onto African Americans themselves.[3] It is hard to interpret her explanation as anything more than self-serving revisionism. As I demonstrate in this essay, the rush to incarcerate was fueled by much less generous motives than the ones Clinton presents. With the Clintons at the helm of the "New Democrats," their strident anticrime policies, like their assault on welfare, reflected a cynical attempt to win back centrist white voters, especially those from Dixie and the south central United States.[4]

A true paradox lies at the heart of the Clinton legacy. Both Hillary and Bill continue to enjoy enormous popularity among African Americans despite the devastating legacy of a presidency that resulted in the impoverishment and incarceration of hundreds of thousands of poor and working-class Black people. Most shockingly, the total

numbers of state and federal inmates grew more rapidly under Bill
Clinton than under any other president, including the notorious Republican drug warriors Richard Nixon, Ronald Reagan, and George
H. W. Bush. This fact alone should at least make one pause before
granting unquestioning fealty to Hillary, but of course there are many
others, including her entry into electoral politics through the 1964
Goldwater campaign, resolute support for the Violent Crime Control
and Law Enforcement Act, race-baiting tactics in the 2008 election,
and close ties to lobbyists for the private prison industry.[5] Nevertheless, until the encounter with BLMM/M4BL protestors in August
2015, few publicly called out the Clintons' shared culpability for our
contemporary prison nation that subjects a third of African American men to a form of correctional control in their lifetime.[6]

The United States' historically unprecedented carceral edifice of
policing and prisons has been long in the making. However, in the
1990s, the Clintons and their allies, as the quintessential "New Democrats," played a crucial role in its expansion. As with their Republican predecessors, punishing America's most vulnerable populations[7]
became an important means to repudiate the democratic upheaval
of the postwar years that toppled statutory Jim Crow and challenged
some of the most enduring social inequities in the US. In the three decades that followed the passage of the Voting Rights Act, the drug war
and its companion legislation, welfare reform, criminalized poor and
working-class populations of color in huge numbers, subjecting many
not only to the "carceral consequences" of voter disfranchisement but
also to permanent exclusion from the legal economy.[8]

While this is often understood as the quotidian cruelty of a brave
neoliberal world, very specific political motives underlay policies of
extreme cruelty and state-sanctioned murder in the late twentieth
century. Although they are rarely mentioned in the same breath, the
escalation of America's drug war in the 1990s and the rise of the Democratic Leadership Council (DLC) and its benighted son Bill Clinton

are all intimately linked. Understanding why tough-on-crime policies and welfare reform became so foundational to the vision of the New Democrats requires a look at the sensibilities that undergirded their strategy for regaining the White House and national power. As the Democratic Party reinvented itself in the aftermath of Ronald Reagan's sweeping electoral victory in 1984, Al From, an aide of Louisiana representative Gillis Long with abiding ties to big business, and Governors Bruce Babbitt (AZ) and Charles Robb (VA) came together with Florida senator Lawton Chiles and congressional representatives Richard Gephardt (MS), Sam Nunn (GA), and James R. Jones (OK) to launch the DLC in February 1985. The DLC's coterie of conservative and centrist politicians, who hailed overwhelmingly from citadels of white discontent in the Sunbelt and Midwest, sought to wrest the party away from its alleged liberal dominance.[9]

In terms of structural changes, they targeted the 1968 reforms to the Democratic Party's nomination process that established interest group–based organizations. By 1982 the Democratic National Committee (DNC) recognized seven different intraparty caucuses modeled on specific demographics, including "women, Blacks, Hispanics, Asians, gays, liberals and business/professionals."[10] The DLC founders wanted to abandon this pluralistic party base, elevate the power of national elected officials, and pursue stronger ties with wealthy corporate donors.[11]

To diagnose the precise causes behind the Democrats' catastrophic loss of every state in the Union to Ronald Reagan in 1984, with the exception of Walter Mondale's home state of Minnesota, the DNC sponsored several research surveys, including one that has been estimated, at that time, to be the most expensive study commissioned in its history. Chair Paul Kirk paid survey researchers Milton Kotler and Nelson Rosenbaum a quarter of a million dollars to conduct a massive survey of five thousand voters. In focus groups, whites from the South and Northern ethnic enclaves described the Democratic

Party as the "give away party," giving white tax money to Blacks and poor people." The explicit racist content of Kotler and Rosenbaum's report proved so embarrassing to Kirk that he suppressed its release and had nearly all of the existing copies destroyed.[12] Nevertheless, the findings made their way into DLC party policy as New Democrat fellow travelers like Thomas and Mary Edsall and Harry McPherson made similar, if more carefully veiled, arguments. McPherson, a former member of the Johnson administration, published a November 1988 op-ed essay in the New York Times entitled simply "How Race Destroyed the Democrats' Coalition."[13]

At the core of this anger about the shift in the Democratic Party was not just "race" as an abstraction, which too often functioned as a polite euphemism, but rather Black people themselves. Another DNC-commissioned study by Stanley Greenberg, who subsequently became a pollster for Clinton in 1992, cited data from Macomb County, a suburb of Detroit, to make this point even more explicitly. "These white Democratic defectors express a profound distaste for Blacks, a sentiment that pervades almost everything they think about government and politics," explained Greenberg. "Blacks constitute the explanation for their [white defectors'] vulnerability and almost everything that has gone wrong in their lives, not being Black is what constitutes being middle class, not being Black is what makes a neighborhood a decent place to live."[14]

Bolstered with polling data and the crisis of the Reagan landslide, the New Democrats searched for ways to aggressively distance themselves from "Blacks" and to entice resentful white swing voters back into the fold. To do this, the New Democrats appropriated hot button issues from the Republican Party, later deemed "dog whistle politics," that invoked the specter of Blackness without directly naming it. While the turn from welfare to work and personal responsibility is often discussed in this respect, equally important is the extensive role played by Bill Clinton and his allies in vastly expanding carceral policies, including the War on Drugs, the federal death penalty, and national funding for policing and prisons in the years after the Reagan and Bush presidencies.[15]

Associated with the DLC's early stirrings, Bill Clinton did not become integrally involved until after Michael Dukakis's presidential defeat in 1988.[16] In a notorious ad campaign that drew on enduring racist imagery, George H. W. Bush won the election by blaming the Massachusetts governor for the brutal rape of a white woman by Willie Horton, a Black prisoner participating in a prison furlough program. Bush advisor Lee Atwater created a vicious media blitz that featured a voice-over description of the assault paired with a menacing black-and-white mugshot of Horton. After contrasting Dukakis's opposition to the death penalty with Bush's ardent support for it, the television spot closed with the words "Weekend Prison Passes—Dukakis on Crime."[17] Atwater's race-baiting appeal proved wildly successful. As legal scholar Jonathan Simon has argued, George H. W. Bush's election "marked the emergence, for the first time, of the war on crime as the primary basis for choosing a president."[18]

Chastened by Dukakis's defeat, Bill Clinton emerged as the Southern golden boy of the New Democrats by 1990. While serving as governor of Arkansas, he became the DLC's first chair outside the Beltway. Clinton traveled nonstop and worked tirelessly to build a national infrastructure that encompassed over two dozen state-level chapters. Two years later, his rousing speech at the DLC's national conference in Cleveland, Ohio, earned him a direct line to the nomination.[19] New Democrat stalwart Sam Nunn's early endorsement played a key role, as did that of lesser known members of the DLC fold, among them African American representatives John Lewis (GA), Mike Espy (MI), William Jefferson (LA), and Floyd Flake (NY). In a depressingly familiar pattern from the Reagan administration, the support of an elite sector of the Black political class helped to legitimize hard-line anticrime policy that proved devastating for low-income populations of color.[20]

Prior to his entrée onto the national stage, Clinton's governorship of Arkansas demonstrated how embracing the death penalty paved the Democrats' road back to power. After a comparatively liberal first term in which he granted more than seventy separate sentencing commutations, Clinton radically reversed his earlier stance after his Republican opponent won largely by smearing him in the eyes of the electorate as considerate of criminals. Upon returning to the governor's mansion in 1982, Clinton parsed out a meager seven additional commutations over a ten-year span, and none for the death penalty. Indeed, in 1992 amid massive press coverage, Bill flew back to Arkansas days before the New Hampshire primary to preside over the execution of Ricky Ray Rector, a Black man convicted of killing a white police officer. Rector had shot himself through the temple, forcing surgeons to remove over three inches of the frontal lobe of his brain. He was so cognitively impacted as a result of the surgery that he set aside the dessert from his last meal to eat after his lethal injection. Rector even told a reporter that he planned to vote for Bill Clinton in the fall.[21]

As the governor of a Southern state, Clinton's execution of Rector was a powerful symbolic act that refuted incumbent president George H. W. Bush's attempt to cast Bill Clinton and his running mate, Al Gore, as soft on crime. In the words of political kingmaker David Garth, Clinton "had someone put to death who had only part of a brain. You can't find them any tougher than that."[22] Far from gratuitous cruelty, Rector's execution and the virulent and racially discriminatory policies that followed it were the ultimate indication that the post–Civil Rights Democratic Party had repudiated its marginal commitment not only to Black equality, but to Black life itself. Between 1994 and 1999, nearly two-thirds of the people sentenced to the federal death penalty were Black—a rate nearly seven times that of their representation in the American population.[23]

Today, the death penalty haunts the edges of American politics, but at the height of the country's rush to mass incarcerate, executions became central to the rightward drift of the Democratic Party. Once in office, Bill Clinton made sixty new crimes eligible for the death penalty and fellow Democrats bragged about their specific additions to the list.[24] Joe Biden mused that "someone asleep for the last twenty years might wake up to think that Republicans were represented by Abbie Hoffman" and the Democrats by J. Edgar Hoover.[25]

As president, Bill Clinton and his allies embarked on a draconian punishment campaign to outflank the Republicans. "I can be nicked a lot, but no one can say that I'm soft on crime," he bragged.[26] Roughly a year and a half after the 1992 Los Angeles Rebellion—at that time, the largest civil disturbance in US history, in which demonstrators took to the streets for six straight days to protest the acquittal of the officers involved in the Rodney King beating—Clinton passed the Violent Crime Control and Law Enforcement Act. At its core, this legislation was a federal "three strikes" bill that established a $30.2 billion Crime Trust Fund to allocate monies for state and municipal police and prison expansion. Like its predecessors, starting with Johnson's Omnibus Crime Control and Safe Streets Act, the federal government provided funding to accelerate punitive policies at all levels of governance. Specific provisions included monies for placing a hundred thousand new police on the streets, the expansion of death-penalty-eligible crimes, lifetime imprisonment for people who committed a third violent federal felony offense with two prior state or federal felony convictions, gang "enhancements" in sentencing for federal defendants, allowing children as young as thirteen to be prosecuted as adults in special cases, and the Violence Against Women Act.[27]

Hillary strongly supported this legislation and stood resolutely behind her husband's punishment campaign. "We need more police, we need more and tougher prison sentences for repeat offenders," Hillary declared in 1994. "The 'three strikes and you're out' for violent offenders has to be part of the plan. We need more prisons to keep violent offenders for as long as it takes to keep them off the streets," she added.[28] Elsewhere, she remarked, "We will finally be able to say, loudly and clearly, that for repeat, violent, criminal offenders: three strikes and you're out."[29]

Like his notorious Republican predecessors, Clinton imposed a toxic mix of punishment and withdrawal of social welfare, but with a difference. The Democratic president actually implemented these policies on a much larger scale than the Republican New Right. According to *New Jim Crow* author Michelle Alexander, "Far from resisting the emergence of the new caste system" that Ronald Reagan had codified into law through the Anti-Drug Abuse Acts of 1986 and 1988, "Clinton escalated the drug war beyond what conservatives had imagined possible a decade earlier."[30]

In the 1980s and 1990s, incarceration became de facto urban policy for impoverished communities of color in America's cities. State and federal legislation imposed mandatory minimums, denied public housing to whole families if any member was suspected of a drug crime, expanded federal death-penalty-eligible crimes, and imposed harsh parole restrictions. Ultimately, authorities subjected multiple generations of America's most vulnerable people, including drug users, Black and Brown residents, and the impoverished to draconian prison sentences and lifelong social and economic marginality.[31] The carceral effects of the New Democrats' competition with the Republicans vastly increased the ranks of the incarcerated. State and federal prisons imprisoned more people under the Clintons' watch than under any previous administration. During his two terms the inmate population grew from roughly 1.3 million to 2 million, and the number of executions to ninety-eight by 1999.[32] Significantly, the Democratic president even refused to support the Congressional Black Caucus's proposed Racial Justice Act, which would have prevented discriminatory application of the death penalty.[33]

Despite this terrible record of racialized punishment for political gain, the Clintons' peculiar ability to reinvent themselves has erased memory of many of their past misdeeds. This is nowhere truer than within the African American community, in which a combination of Bill Clinton's high-profile Black political appointments, his obvious comfort in the presence of Black people, and the cultural symbolism of his saxophone performance on Arsenio Hall's talk show has severely distorted the New Democrats' true legacy for the Black majority. After all, Toni Morrison, African American Nobel Laureate for literature, embraced Bill Clinton as America's "first Black president," even if only in jest.

At a deeper structural level, the constraints of the two-party system have resulted in Black Americans' political capture inside the Democratic Party, in which no viable electoral alternative exists. Frederick Douglass said of the party of Lincoln during Reconstruction, "The Republican Party is the ship, all else is the sea." And so it is with Democrats in the era of mass incarceration. Equally important is the sharp class polarization inside the African American community in which a select group of Black elites understand their fate as wholly bound up with the leadership of the Democratic Party. The Clinton presidency is a cautionary tale in this respect. The couple's close relationships with Vernon Jordan and other Black insiders offered an illusion of access that superseded any real concern for how hard-line anticrime, drug war, and welfare policies affected poor and working-class African Americans. As the movement against state-sanctioned violence and for Black lives grows, it is important to remember that proximity to power rarely equals real power.

In American politics we so often live in an eternal present. Forgotten are the days of the DLC, which was dismantled in 2011 at the close of President Barack Obama's first term. In many respects, the DLC had become archaic, precisely because contemporary Democrats have so fully incorporated, and even expanded, the bitter fruit of the Reagan revolution. Former Federal Reserve chairman and Ayn Rand enthusiast Alan Greenspan once described Bill Clinton as "the best Republican president we've had in a while."[34] More recently, Barack Obama praised Ronald Reagan for correcting "the excesses of the 1960s and 1970s."[35] As both parties have engaged in a steady march to the right over the past three decades, it is not surprising that the Clintons have done little more than offer half-hearted *mea culpas* about their role in the drug war and mass incarceration. In July 2015, Bill Clinton went before the National Association for the Advancement of Color People's 106th annual convention to admit that his federal drug and anticrime policy made the problem of mass incarceration worse, especially at the state level. Many journalists interpreted his candor cynically as advance preparation for his wife's presidential campaign of 2016.[36] As in so many things the Clintons have done, even their disavowals appear to be self-serving. Hillary's explanation that a crime wave inside low-income communities of color motivated her husband's escalation of domestic wars on drugs and crime hides the Clintons' shared role in capitulating to racist rhetoric and policy in the 1990s. Indeed, they used the drug war, and mass incarceration more broadly, as a powerful political tool to rebuild conservative white support for the Democratic Party. It is only because the experiences of the incarcerated and the poor have been so profoundly erased that the Clintons can be thought of as liberals (racial or otherwise) in any respect.[37]

As we approach the 2016 election, it would be good to remember the human consequences of the Clintons' "tough on crime" stance, and how Hillary has tried to replicate this strategy of "strength and experience" again and again to prove her appropriateness as both a female presidential contender and a blue dog Democrat. Candidate Clinton has embraced hardness as political qualification, as evidenced by her proclamation "We came, we saw, he died," about the killing of Muammar Gaddafi; her threat to obliterate Iran; or her embellished Bosnian sniper story.[38] As mainstream feminist icon, Hillary has more in common with Britain's Iron Lady Margaret Thatcher or the European Union's austerity champion Angela Merkel than her beloved Eleanor Roosevelt. If the history of the War on Drugs is any indicator, however, outstripping Republican belligerence from the right will not end well for the rest of us.

PART III

RACIAL CAPITALISM AND BLACK LIVES

CHAPTER 6

FERGUSON'S INHERITANCE

N ear the one-year anniversary of Michael Brown's killing, within days of the anniversary of the Watts Rebellion, we are invited to reflect on the connection between state repression and African American mobilization past and present. Each generation has a moment when its members share an instance of collective experience that is forever etched into their memory. For the Civil Rights Movement and Black Power generation, it was unquestionably the open-casket funeral of Emmett Till.[1] The disfigured remains of this fourteen-year-old boy became a mirror in which Black youth witnessed their most vulnerable selves. The sight was so excruciating that it helped catalyze direct action protests from rural Alabama to the streets of Oakland for nearly a decade and a half. Today, for a broad swath of people ranging in age from those born in the waning years of the Black Power movement through the interstice between the twentieth and twenty-first centuries, this moment was embodied in Ferguson.[2]

The precise calculus of generation is elusive. As Jeff Chang has argued, "Generations are fictions." And yet, we all have a personal and public sense of time that places us within a cohort of history. Whether we use the branding terms "the Hip-Hop Generation" or "Generation X," or the not-for-profit ring of "Millennial Youth," particularly for those of us who came of age under presidents Ronald Reagan

---

* "Ferguson's Inheritance" originally appeared in *Jacobin* (2015). Reprinted with permission.

through Barack Obama, the events in this small municipality outside northern St. Louis were profoundly meaningful. It might even be said that the events of the past year have helped distinguish the post–Civil Rights generations from iconic baby boomers, because the months of mass protest announced what many of us feel is the most pressing domestic political crisis of our time: the emergence of a massive edifice of policing, surveillance, prisons, and punishment that is unprecedented in both US and global history.

Built on the centuries-long substructure of white supremacy, but nurtured in an era of neoliberal retreat and technological advance, this massive state-building project, known alternately as mass incarceration, the new Jim Crow, the prison-industrial complex, or more simply, according to former *New York Times* journalist Chris Hedges, "the world's most advanced police state," has become a defining feature of our times. It is impossible to understand the enormity of the reaction to Michael Brown's murder without recognizing the daunting shadow cast by state repression in the fifty-year aftermath of the modern Civil Rights Movement.[3] Police left Michael Brown's body in the street for nearly five hours, immersed in his own blood. Like the body of Emmett Till, the devastating sight of this murdered youth was intolerable. Word and image spread first to the residents of Canfield Green where he lay and then, through the digital magic of cyber networks, to the rest of the St. Louis metro area, the nation, and the world. Twitter, Instagram, Facebook, and Vine carried the story beyond the city's periphery, ultimately forcing mainstream media to reckon with its gravity.

However, the media blitz focused not on the destruction of a person, but rather of property. The pattern continued in Baltimore, which is another economically devastated city located in the overlapping borderlands between the North and South that failed to attract sustained press coverage until fevered reports of "looting" became the focal point of the television news cycle.[4] Even more important to the impact and longevity of Ferguson as site of protest and mobilization was the ingenuity and commitment of the protesters who refused to leave—even when confronted with tanks, military hardware, and clouds of tear gas. Instead they started publicly counting the days of sustained resistance and in so doing announced to St. Louis County and the rest of the world that they would not stop until they had attained justice for Mike Brown and the many other men, women, and children shot down by police. The protest continues.

What made Ferguson into such a watershed moment was not simply the terror-inspiring image of police impunity, but that a large cohort of African American youth decided to fight back and confront state authorities. Along the way, they developed allies and "coconspirators," in the words of Black Lives Matter cofounder Alicia Garza, from different ethnic and racial communities, more-affluent cities across the country, and international solidarity groups.[5] This was nowhere truer than with Palestinians who tweeted from the West Bank in early August with instructions about how to mitigate the effects of tear gas. International exchange continued and deepened in the months that followed, as the twin threads of Boycott, Divestment, and Sanctions against Israel and the burgeoning African American–led movement against state-sanctioned violence inside the United States intertwined.

During "Ferguson October," activists launched a sustained organizing effort that spanned a four-day weekend meant to draw support from across the country in a Black Power–style remix of Freedom Summer.[6] After attending a hip-hop gathering including performances by local and nationally known artists such as Tef Poe, T-Dubb-O, and Dead Prez, I wrote the following words that captured for me the sheer force and beauty of the genesis of a new protest era unlike anything I had experienced firsthand:

> I have no words to express what is happening in Ferguson. In the name of Michael Brown, a beautiful Black storm against state violence is brewing so dense it has created a gravity of its own, draw-

ing in people from all over the US, from centers of wealth and privilege to this city whose most prosperous years were a century ago. It looks explicitly not only to St. Louis City and County police and other municipal law enforcement, but also to the imperial wars in the Middle East as sites of murder and trauma. The call repeated over and over is Stokely Carmichael's: "Organize, Organize, Organize." And this growing youth movement has all the ancestral sweetness of kinship. In the words of a local Hip-Hop artist/activist, "Our grandparents would be proud of us."

Local police were not the only focus. Corporate chains Walmart and QuikTrip became flash points of conflict, even more so than the small businesses that the local news identified in the sensationalized coverage of looting in early August. Protesters frequently gathered outside the Department of Justice in St. Louis, while flash mobs appeared regularly throughout the metro area. Consistently, activists sponsored three or four simultaneous direct actions at different locations every day, ranging from flash mobs at Walmart to protesters whistling "FTP" in Morse code outside the police station.

Organized actions abounded that would have warmed the heart of Saul Alinsky, like the beautiful baritone voice, replete with a full operatic chorus, that preempted the St. Louis Symphony's performance of Brahms's *Requiem*. Demonstrators adapted the lyrics from the United Mine Workers' anthem, "Which Side Are You On," from the deadly labor strikes in the coal mines of Harlan County, West Virginia.[7]

Which side are you on friends?
Which side are you on?
Justice for Mike Brown friends.
Justice for us all.

Afterwards, a multiracial group arranged strategically throughout the theater shouted "Black Lives Matter" over and over, a cappella. As they sang, protesters threw long, black-and-white cloth banners over the balcony, scrolled with signs and drawings including "Requiem for Mike Brown 1996 to 2014," "Racism Lives Here" with an arrow pointing straight down to the skyline's Gateway Arch, and "Come Join the Movement" adorned with a bright yellow shining sun.[8]

While local residents formed the core of this wave of protest, constant outside attention and migration of people to support this movement of organized resistance played a crucial role. Black Lives Matter sponsored its own "freedom rides" bringing nearly six hundred people of African descent from eighteen cities, including New York, Los Angeles, Toronto, Chicago, Austin, Atlanta, Winston-Salem, and Tucson. In addition to Black Lives Matter, the faith-based not-for-profit group People Improving Communities through Organizing (PICO), headquartered in Washington, DC, provided support staff and resources from the earliest days of the protest. PICO organizers, in fact, helped stage a Moral Monday protest by local clergy in which they offered the sacrament of "repentance" to Ferguson police officers.[9] To powerful effect, the clergy and other demonstrators called out the names of people who had been killed by the police, and rhythmically shouted after each victim, "Repent." "Mike Brown—Repent," "VonDerrit Myers Jr.—Repent," "Renisha McBride—Repent." And so on for hours.

Protesters and ordinary people created and maintained memorials in the place where Michael Brown's body lay, set up camp in front of the Ferguson police headquarters on South Florissant, and marched regularly along what a local minister called "The Jericho Road" stretching from Canfield Drive to the edge of Dellwood, a neighboring majority-Black municipality. Demonstrators staffed pickets in front of the Ferguson police station for twenty-one hours a day, sharing rides and food as they crafted their own movement culture. Direct action protests like these later spread to the Shaw district of South St. Louis, following the murder of eighteen-year-old

VonDerrit Myers Jr., who was shot six times in the legs and once in the face after a policeman employed by a private security firm mistook Myers's sandwich for a gun.

As this mosaic of struggle indicates, over the past year Ferguson and the greater St. Louis metro area has become a laboratory and genesis point for a new generation of activists against state-sanctioned violence. It has also helped inspire a new wave of twenty-first-century iterations of Black Power both for local youth and for those across North America. These efforts, and the national and international press and social media coverage they generated, marked a turning point, a before and after, in which perception changed. Solidarity protests in New York, Los Angeles, and smaller cities throughout the country immediately followed, and in the process, a national collective memory was forged. This is not to say that what happened in Ferguson was something entirely new; it certainly was not. Anti-police brutality protest has a long history, and a small segment of its most recent past could be traced as far back as the late 1970s and 1980s, to the police murders of Eula Love, Eleanor Bumpers, Michael Stewart, and many, many others.

But to understand the social dynamics of Ferguson and the many months of protest that have followed in an era of both cybernetic networks and of the "Arab Spring," we need to look to more recent struggles. The campaigns seeking justice for Oscar Grant, Sean Bell, Troy Davis, Sakia Gunn, and Trayvon Martin are Ferguson's direct lineal antecedents. In fact, the events in St. Louis represented the culmination both of long-standing forces of repression and criminalization, as well as of resistance.

REBELLION AND REPRESSION

In a speech at the National Press Club in 1986—during Ronald Reagan's second presidential term, on the eve of the Iran Contra hearings—

James Baldwin reflected on the importance of history and of America's discomfort in reckoning with the full burden of its meaning:

> One of the things that has always afflicted the American reality and the American vision is this aversion to history. History is not something you read about in a book; history is not even the past, it's the present, because everybody operates, whether or not we know it, out of assumptions which are produced only, and only by, our history.[10]

Locating the exact origins of the current epidemic of police violence is not an easy task. Its causes are many and cumulative, ranging over a broad swath of time. As Robin D. G. Kelley and others have pointed out, the link between race and criminalization in the United States is at least as old as the Atlantic slave trade itself. Slave patrols from the antebellum era, and convict leasing and the organized system of terror in the postbellum and segregated South, as well as the turn toward Jim Crow justice in the years after the arrest of the Scottsboro Boys are all part of the long history of race and criminalization.

Equally important to this history is private as well as state violence, as seen in the brutal act of racial vigilantism that killed Emmett Till with impunity. But to understand the nature of Ferguson protest, it is essential to look at the major developments of the last half century that are often elided or ignored in popular media. Paramount to this history is the state response to the popular mobilizations of the postwar era and the criminalization of exactly the kinds of youth who participated in the popular upheavals of the 1960s urban rebellions and Black Power movement. It is in this moment of reaction that the seeds of contemporary police militarization were sown, as well as the divisions within the African American community, which ultimately have made it difficult to organize in a unified way until very recently.

There are many examples to illustrate this point. Take California, a state that has helped lead the expansion of America's incarceration rate. The history of the Golden State generally, and Los Angeles specifically, is essential to understanding how America has become a "prison nation" in the years of *reconquista* (reconquest) following mass protest and civil unrest. California is home to Oakland's Black Panther Party for Self-Defense, the Watts Rebellion, and the law enforcement commando unit SWAT. These historical developments are not coincidental, but directly related. California has the largest prison population in the United States, which in turn has the largest prison population in the world. Strikingly, 70 percent of the state's prisoners come from Southern California, and the city of Los Angeles alone has the ominous distinction of housing the largest number of urban prisoners on the planet. In 2000, California incarcerated African Americans at a rate nearly four and a half times their representation in the general population, and Latinos at a rate three times as high. To paraphrase Cornel West, race really does matter to this history.

High incarceration rates of populations of color are not a recent development. As evidence of this practice it is key to note that California is part of "Aztlán," or "occupied land," seized by United States after its war with Mexico in 1848. During the lead-up to the Civil War and Reconstruction, the state caged significant numbers of Native Americans who were then leased out to public and private employers. It also had one of the highest rates of lynching, not exclusively as a form of racial control, but as a system of frontier justice for punishing transgression and social crime. By the turn of the twentieth century, California already had the highest rate of incarceration in the country. To put it bluntly, California has been putting large numbers of people in prison for a long time (especially those who are Black, brown, Indigenous, and poor). But in the late twentieth century, this tendency vastly accelerated, and the state began to export some of its most brutal methods, including SWAT, gang injunctions, and gang enhancements, to the rest of the country.

But African Americans and Latinos fought back against these oppressive structures, past and present. The Watts Rebellion, or the Watts riot as it is more popularly known, was the largest civil disturbance in US history up until that point and was occasioned, unsurprisingly, by an incident of police brutality.[11] In August of 1965, five days after the signing of the Voting Rights Act, the community of Watts in Los Angeles, California, erupted in violent protest over the police beating and jailing of a twenty-one-year-old African American youth and the abuse of his mother. Watts surprised the rest of the country because it broke out in a moment of victory: the culmination of the Southern Civil Rights Movement's push for civil and electoral inclusion. For the first time in history, all Black women and men in regions throughout the United States won full voting rights, with the federal government guaranteeing systematic mechanisms of enforcement. In essence, the final legal plank in the Southern system of Jim Crow had been demolished.

Nevertheless, within several days after the passage of this historic legislation and the dispatch of federal voting rights marshals into the South, a cataclysmic urban rebellion erupted in an impoverished and largely ignored Black migrant community on the West Coast. The Watts Rebellion signaled that, despite the dismantling of regional, legally enforced segregation, African Americans throughout Northern and Western cities faced profound forms of racial discrimination untouched by the decade-long mobilization in the American South. Paramount among these was the constant abuse of police power: arbitrary arrest, shootings of unarmed people, harassment, beatings and murders of children, and, in New York, the first generation of stop-and-frisk laws.

Watts was in many ways emblematic of the problems of Black urban poor and working-class people, then and now. Located in the outer reaches of South Central Los Angeles, the neighborhood was a direct portal for recent migrants from the American South. The forces of housing segregation and redlining contributed to overcrowding, with a quarter of a million people hemmed into an area of less than three square miles. In fact, Martin Luther King argued that Watts faced the worst overcrowding in the nation. Contained within strictly drawn boundaries, law enforcement over-policed and underserved this impoverished area in South LA. Not surprisingly, while African Americans made up 98 percent of residents, the police department was nearly all white and drawn from distant white enclaves.[12]

Perhaps more than any other neighborhood of its time, Watts embodied what two eminent social scientists have called "American Apartheid." Like the other urban rebellions of the 1960s and 1970s, the residents of Watts registered their anger at police, and "the racial state" more broadly, by taking to the streets. The rebellion lasted six days, from August 11 to August 17, 1965. It left thirty-four people dead and property losses totaling over $40 million. Unfortunately, officials called in the National Guard to quell the disturbance, and it along with other branches of law enforcement caused the overwhelming majority of deaths and injuries. Looked at from hindsight, the Watts riot's long-term causes, like those of the scores of other urban rebellions that swept through American cities in the 1960s to which Ferguson has been compared, hinged on two central issues: the political economy of race and the long-standing history of systemic police abuse and criminalization of Africans Americans. The urban rebellions and their political expression, "Black Power," responded to what Bayard Rustin understood as the more complex problems of "unemployment, housing and education" in Northern and Western cities.[13]

Few places embodied the devastating effects of the overlapping systems of Northern (and Western) racial discrimination more than Watts. Watts was an urban portal for the poorest and most recent migrants from the South, and Eldridge Cleaver remembered his hometown as "a place of shame." As newcomers settled at the social margins of the United States' second-largest city, they faced intense racial and class segregation, miserable schools, and large-scale joblessness. A hostile and overwhelmingly white police force engaged in routine traffic stops of motorists of color, beatings, and harassment. Given the collective Black suffering in South LA, the chance to actually fight back directly against these conditions thrilled many residents.

Watts became emblematic of a new era of militancy that looked to armed self-defense, direct confrontation with the state, and economic redistribution as political imperatives. Indeed, many have argued that it initiated the new era of Black Power politics. Particularly for the young, the poor, and the economically marginal, Watts was a deeply meaningful rebellion that called attention to the everyday effects of racism and white supremacy. It made visible the problems of the urban North and its forgotten populations that had largely been untouched by the gains of the Southern Civil Rights Movement. And while many journalists and popular histories have denounced these so-called "riots" as tragic and destructive failures that destroyed liberalism, it is important to recognize how profoundly they influenced US social welfare policy. During the Black Power era, postwar redistributive programs responded directly to the hundreds of thousands of people taking to the streets in protest. It is doubtful that without this massive wave of civil unrest sharp increases in federal funding for higher education targeted to students of color, community action programs, small business loans for "minority contractors," and, more broadly, the expansion of social welfare infrastructure to impoverished populations of color would have been implemented. And while this remains an "inconvenient truth" to many, the specter of large-scale property destruction was indeed integral to protest tactics that won major concessions. Over the course of a single decade, from 1960 to 1970, state spending on housing and other urban policy issues expanded from $600 million to over $3 billion. Indeed, the federal government created a whole new agency to deal with the so-called "urban crisis": the Department of Housing and Urban Development.[14]

For many Americans, this account challenges some of the most cherished understandings of the heroes and villains of the 1960s. So much of our current national memory focuses on the triumphant efforts of an interracial, nonviolent movement that overturned the inequities of Jim Crow. But if you really want to understand the problems facing today's African American communities, it is the history of regions outside the South that are most instructive. It is the urban North and West that directly anticipate the problems that we see today. Although our national post-racial narrative focuses almost entirely on the elimination of legal segregation, it is actually these lesser-known histories that best explain the problems of structural racism, police violence, and mass incarceration facing successive generations in the years after the Voting Rights Act's passage.

As many young people look back on the social movements of the 1960s and 1970s, they see only defeats. However, from the point of view of law enforcement and the state more broadly, this period represented an era of unprecedented delegitimization. It is hard to overestimate the anger and fear that militant Black community mobilization inspired among authorities. City and state governments understood Watts, and the urban rebellions more generally, as apocalyptic destruction that should be punished. Like the iron fist and the velvet glove, the war on crime and the war on poverty were historically intertwined. Indeed, in 1966, a year after Watts, an ambitious former actor who had recently switched from the Democratic to the Republican Party was elected governor of California on a law-and-order platform opposing the antiwar movement and urban uprisings. Significantly, Ronald Reagan won by capturing a majority of white, unionized households despite his opposition to organized labor. This same man would later became notorious for expanding America's devastating war(s) on drugs in the 1980s. Lesser known, however, is how a decade before, Governor Reagan's hard-line stance prompted his counterpart in New York, the historically liberal Nelson Rockefeller—who had equally grand national ambitions—to reverse his earlier public-health approach to drug use and to launch the most draconian anti-drug laws in the country in 1973.

So as the country arced to the right, the lesson that law enforcement drew from Watts was not that it needed to consider how its systematic mistreatment of African Americans had caused such large-scale destruction. No. Nor that greater community input was needed either. Instead, authorities responded to what they defined as an irrational wave of disorder by creating new and more repressive forms of policing that were modeled explicitly on American military campaigns abroad.[15] During and after Watts, the LAPD arrested more than four thousand people and conducted large-scale house-to-house searches. In addition, law enforcement worked to acquire military-grade hardware and elite tactical units as part of its "counterinsurgency" campaigns against urban protests and Black and Brown Power organizations.

This pre-history is almost entirely left out of the mainstream coverage of the events in St. Louis, Baltimore, and other recent sites of protest. At most, we hear a discussion of how the 1033 Program of the National Defense Authorization Act funded the adoption of surplus military hardware by police departments. But there is rarely a sustained discussion of the War on Drugs, much less the bombastic response of law enforcement to the highly politicized urban uprisings of the 1960s that are Ferguson's direct lineal antecedents. The events in Ferguson and other parts of the country cannot be understood without considering state repression against the mass political upheaval of the 1960s. Large-scale arrests and authoritarian response by police during Watts paved the way for this new repressive era marked by federal and local cooperation in law enforcement and the widespread use of military hardware for crowd control.[16] The political backlash against Watts, subsequent urban rebellions, and the Black Power movement more broadly are crucial to understanding the rise not only of bipartisan support for law and order, but of the contemporary carceral state.

Understanding the choice of the term "carceral state" requires some context. Its roots lie in a parallel movement in the university that has anticipated mass protest in the streets over police killings and subsequently flourished as protests have grown. In the early 2000s, as a number of graduate students completed their dissertations on the Black Panther Party and other radical movements of the post-war period, it became clear that the story could not be told without a parsing of the dynamics of state repression, policing, and surveillance.[17] Michel Foucault first popularized the term "carceral" with the publication of *Discipline and Punish* in the mid-1970s. More recently, American academics have embraced the term "carceral," from the Latin *carceralis* or *carcer*, of or belonging to prison, in order to identify a wide range of punitive state actions. These include aggressive policing; racist criminalization; moral panics and targeted punishment campaigns against illicit or informal economies; modes of incarceration across vectors of age, race, sex, gender conformity, and legal status; courts, prosecution, and parole; jails, prisons, asylums, and other forms of social immobilization; the school-to-prison pipeline; border patrol and immigrant detention; public and private surveillance; and restrictive and means-tested social service policies.

This broad and capacious view of punishment has been chosen in order to analyze not only mass incarceration, but a more seismic shift from a redistributive to a punitive state in which carcerality, like the militarization of policing, saturates even the social welfare functions of governance in the late twentieth century. Punishment is not unique to America's past half century. Indeed, it is constitutive of a settler society born of land expropriation, native genocide, and enslavement of Africans. However, since the passage of landmark civil-rights legislation in the mid-1960s, we have witnessed an unprecedented intensification of the carceral state. Significantly, after decades of ever more punitive campaigns, its most concrete expression—the police killings of unarmed people who are overwhelmingly of African descent—has catalyzed mass protest. It is a truism of left social history that repression breeds resistance. But the real question is not if, but when? And what conditions make this possible? The decades-long accumulation of police powers, and at a more foundational level, the elevation of punishment as the solution to all social problems, is indeed daunting. This is why Ferguson has been so meaningful to us all. To watch young people literally face down tanks and protest twenty-one hours a day in the quest for justice for one of their peers has shown us all that fighting back is possible.

Nested within the Ferguson movement are a number of important issues, including the imperative of organizing against racial capitalism. Fighting the militarization of police is crucial, but equally important is confronting the problem of "policing for profit" as described in the recent Department of Justice report, which found everything wrong about the Ferguson Police Department, *except* the actual shooting of Michael Brown by Darren Wilson.[18] However, the DOJ did provide a systematic account of how Ferguson and St. Louis County more broadly financed themselves, to borrow Toni Morrison's phrase, "on the backs of Blacks." This larger problem, that many have dubbed "racial capitalism," is key to understanding not only the Ferguson protests, but the wars on drugs, gangs, and crime that predated it. Civil forfeiture has created an incentive structure for local police departments all over the country.[19] Once a person is accused—not convicted—of a drug crime, their property can be legally seized. That includes everything from the content of their wallets, to a watch on their wrist, to a car, house, or mobile phone. From 1984 to 1990, at the height of the wars on drugs and gangs, the LAPD expected to receive $20 million from forfeited property. We are dealing with a system in which racism pays. To push back against this, we need the kind of scrutiny that has been focused on St. Louis County to be applied to policing practices across the country. And, more importantly, we need to organize mass movements against the deadly mixture of profit and racism that has incentivized mass arrests and killings throughout our history.

In addition to highlighting the wages of racial capitalism and anti-black racism, the Ferguson rebellions demonstrate that each generation confronts the overarching structure of power in its own way. One of the most remarkable elements in Ferguson has been watching a whole cohort of new activists emerge within weeks of Michael Brown's murder. Strikingly, a significant number of protesters and organizers had felony convictions and spoke openly about their effects, thereby giving voice to those most directly injured by the domestic warfare against drugs, gangs, and crime. Given how the shaming process around incarceration has helped inhibit organizing, this is a significant and hopeful development.

Similarly, women with a range of backgrounds have served at the forefront of this movement, as have self-identified Black queer and gender-variant people. Black Lives Matter, whose hashtag was founded in 2013 and later expanded to local organizing committees throughout the country, has foregrounded not only the need to stop arbitrary arrest, murder, and detention by law enforcement, but to think about the central role of gender identity and sexuality in how we value life itself.

Too often, the killings of Black girls and women, Latinx, Native, and gender-nonconforming populations of color, who are the single most vulnerable group to police and vigilante murder, have not received the attention and solidarity efforts that they deserve. Black Lives Matter has incorporated some of the language and iconography of the Black Power movement, but has expanded its parameters to reckon fully with the tensions and contradictions inside our communities around the intimate and intraracial questions of sexuality and gender. This is very important, and if we only search for charismatic male leadership as our model of social activism, then much of what is new and vibrant is not only lost, but rendered invisible.

Scholars and researchers also have a role to play in the growing movement against state-sanctioned violence. The Black Panthers "started with a study group," and throughout their history, intellectual production and research were key to how they conceptualized and developed new forms of social action from delegitimizing the police to using breakfast programs and liberation schools for political education. Both Black Studies and the Panthers are steeped in this tradition of intellectual engagement as political praxis, and we can learn a lot by drawing on their rich tradition in our present moment.

One of our biggest problems is that we do not know enough about even the most basic and important facts of what law enforcement has done throughout the country. How many people have the police fatally shot over the past ten years? Estimates are as high as ten thousand, but no one really knows because the federal government does not compile this data in any systematic way. So much of the history of police and state-sanctioned violence in the United States remains undocumented. Scholars and researchers need to work with local activist groups and develop tools for recovering this history in rural areas, small municipalities, suburbs, and larger cities. Equally important is looking for historical precedent to understand both the current tools of repression and of resistance. To quote Malcolm X, "Of all our studies, history is the best qualified to reward our research."[20]

CHAPTER 7

PAYING FOR PUNISHMENT

Opposition to mass incarceration and the War on Drugs has lately become fashionable. The Koch brothers, Grover Norquist, and Newt Gingrich are lining up with the NAACP, ACLU, and Van Jones to support criminal justice reform. Many assume that budget savings are driving this newfound consensus. But understanding de-carceration only through the lens of cost cutting has a major blind spot. America's contemporary system of policing, courts, imprisonment, and parole doesn't just absorb money. It also makes money through asset forfeiture, lucrative public contracts from private service providers, and by directly extracting revenue and unpaid labor from populations of color and the poor. In states and municipalities throughout the country, the criminal justice system defrays costs by forcing prisoners and their families to pay for punishment. It also allows private service providers to charge outrageous fees for everyday needs such as telephone calls. As a result, people facing even minor criminal charges can easily find themselves trapped in a self-perpetuating cycle of debt, criminalization, and incarceration.

Thanks to the contemporary activism of the Black Lives Matter Movement, Black Youth Project 100, the Dream Defenders, and hundreds of Ferguson and Baltimore protestors, as well as the long-standing work of activist intellectuals such as Angela Davis, Ruth Wilson Gilmore, Heather Ann Thompson, and Michelle Alexander, many

---

* "Paying for Punishment" originally appeared in the *Boston Review* (2016). Reprinted with permission.

Americans are acquainted with the horrors of police killings and mass incarceration. Lesser known are the devastating economic consequences of the leviathan of policing, courts, bail, jails, prosecution, prisons, probation, and parole. In an era of fiscal austerity and crisis, mass incarceration has enabled private contractors, municipalities, counties, and states to make money off large numbers of America's most vulnerable residents. The historical roots of these extractive practices stretch far back in the American past.[1]

• • •

The promise of boundless opportunity has been a persistent theme in the United States' self-conception, from the mobility of Jacksonian democracy to the enduring belief in "the American dream," a concept first named in 1931 and celebrated ever since.[2] Central to this narrative is Congress's outlawing of debtors' prison in 1833. Twelve states followed suit between 1821 and 1849. The young country's encouragement of greater adventurousness contrasted sharply with mother England's draconian poor laws, which enforced the poverty for which they ostensibly compensated. Unleashing the appetite for capital investment and experimentation in America required forgiving bankruptcy so that potential entrepreneurs could start over. But like so many American institutions, debt forgiveness—and the social mobility it enabled—applied almost exclusively to native-born white men.[3] Nonwhite populations faced land divestment, chattel slavery, and disproportionate incarceration, followed by a subsequent regime of debt peonage and forced labor. Prisons throughout the country—including in the antebellum urban North and parts of the Midwest—used convict labor, an extractive system that evolved into an even more brutal racial form in the post-emancipation South.[4]

Traveling through the Black Belt in the 1890s, W. E. B. Du Bois described a fertile, if broken, landscape plagued by the upward redistribution of wealth. "A pall of debt hangs over the beautiful land," he wrote in *The Souls of Black Folk*. "The merchants are in debt to the wholesalers, the planters are in debt to the merchants, the tenants owe the planters, and the laborers bow and bend beneath the burden of it all."[5] The Thirteenth Amendment, which abolished slavery and involuntary servitude "except as a punishment for crime" enabled the widespread use of debt peonage and convict leasing. This resulted in the deaths of tens of thousands of African Americans between the 1870s and the 1940s, exceeding by a significant magnitude the number who died from lynching. At its very worst, nearly one in four leased convicts died from a mix of overwork, malnutrition, and unsafe working conditions.[6]

State, county, and municipal government played an essential role in the development of these coercive post-emancipation labor practices, which used debt as the pretext for de facto re-enslavement. Criminalization of vagrancy, loitering, quitting a job, petty theft, and even talking loudly in public could result in incarceration for Blacks, accompanied by exorbitant fines and court costs. White employers paid off these debts and in return forced victims to work for years without pay under horrendous conditions. African Americans had no legal recourse to contest such practices, and employers took advantage by imposing additional debt for land use, seed, livestock, food, and other staples. The result was a newly freed population ensnared in an endless cycle of debt, forced labor, and worker abuse that recreated, in the words of Pulitzer Prize–winning author Douglas Blackmon, "slavery by another name."[7]

This extractive system was central to the Southern economy under "Redemption" and Jim Crow. Indeed, debt peonage, chain gangs, and convict leasing enabled the economic resurrection of the region and continued well into the Progressive Era. The city of Atlanta, the crown jewel of the industrial New South, was rebuilt with red brick fashioned by Black convict labor. Public works—roads, aqueducts, bridges—and private residences benefited from this forced labor system enabled by criminalization of large portions of the African American community, including women and children. James W. English, a primary shareholder in the Chattahoochee Brick Company who served as a future police chief and mayor of Atlanta, leased more than a thousand convicts to work in his Georgia brickyards. Similarly, many of the Gilded Age industries of the South—including not only construction but also agriculture and mining—used convict labor to amass wealth.[8]

• • •

Too often the South is understood as exceptional, but the process of racial divestment was national in scope. Financial predation extended beyond the geographical reach of legal segregation and found a new vehicle in racially discriminatory practices such as blockbusting (in which realtors overcharged Black renters and home buyers), redlining, and subprime lending. It also persisted in the criminal justice system in ways that have been made visible by mass protests in Ferguson in response to the August 2014 police shooting of Michael Brown. Sustained activism prompted the federal government and journalists to investigate the town and its woes. Further inquiry revealed interlocking webs of public and private predation that relied on courts and police to garner revenue from Black residents through excessive ticketing as well as the levying of court fees and fines. Today the small municipality north of St. Louis has come to exemplify the dangers of racial profiteering. But while it is extreme, Ferguson is far from an isolated case; many jurisdictions extract money through law enforcement and the court system.

Contemporary extractive methods rely on two interrelated sources of debt: private debt and criminal justice debt, also known as legal financial obligations (LFOs). The former, which pays out to private companies, has a way of generating the latter, which pays out to both private companies and public institutions. Private debt is familiar to most of us. It can easily and quickly be incurred from auto loans, mortgages, extortionary payday loans (frequently the creditors of last resort for low-income people), credit card charges, and medical bills. Private lenders or, more commonly, debt collection companies can in some cases bypass bankruptcy proceedings and take non-paying debtors directly to civil court. A recent report from ProPublica shows just how common civil suits for debt collection are. For instance, sixty-six thousand such suits were brought in Newark alone between the years of 2008 and 2012. Defendants in such suits are overwhelmingly African American. In St. Louis, Chicago, and Newark, majority-Black neighborhoods suffer court judgments for debt collection at twice the rate of majority-white neighborhoods. In Jennings, Missouri, a 90 percent Black city next door to Ferguson, there was more than one court judgment for every four residents. The effect is far-reaching; five of the eight city council members of Jennings have been sued over debt.[9]

Legal judgments were not always the norm. Zealous private collectors began popularizing the use of municipal and county courts in the 1990s, and the practice has since grown. Collection agencies aggressively purchase consumer, medical, and student debt for pennies on the dollar and sue for much smaller amounts than banks do.[10] If the debt remained in the hands of major banks dealing in billions of dollars' worth of transactions every day, small-time debtors might be too unimportant to attract legal attention. But collection agencies specialize in suing large numbers of people for relatively little money, making escape that much more difficult. That people of color are vastly more likely to face court proceedings than are white people with the same income reflects both racial discrimination and the stark wealth gap. Black families, on average, have one-tenth the wealth of white families and Latinos have roughly one-eighth. This wealth gap is a result of the long and continuous history of legalized dispossession via slavery, Jim Crow, forced labor, and myriad racial disparities in housing, education, employment, lending, and incarceration. Consequently, many African Americans have been prevented from building the assets that might insulate them from life's emergencies, resulting in debt and legal hazard that itself generates further opportunities for extraction.[11]

One such opportunity arises when defendants in civil suits do not show up for court dates. In such cases, they can be charged with contempt, failure to appear in court, or disobeying a court order, and judges can issue arrest warrants accompanied by steep fines.[12] According to The Marshall Project, many private debtors are forced to "pay or stay," trapped in jail until they post bond or pay their creditors. Upon arrest they, like all criminal defendants, begin to accrue a second—arguably more calamitous—debt from the justice system itself.[13]

Criminal justice debt is an unwieldy set of financial obligations consisting of fines, fees, and restitution payments. Fines are imposed during sentencing for infractions such as speeding. Fees comprise a broad and capacious category covering charges levied by public and private entities. Costs are racked up at every stage of the process: jail booking fees and per diems for pretrial detention, bail investigation fees, costs of drug and DNA testing, court costs and felony surcharges, public defender application costs and recoupment fees (issued directly to the state, not to the lawyers themselves), and the list goes on. Then there is restitution, which mandates cash payments to victims for personal and property damage. Forty-one states also charge offenders for the cost of imprisonment itself, and forty-four states charge for costs of probation and parole.[14] To make matters worse, the overwhelming majority of the states with the largest prison populations charge "poverty penalties" by imposing additional costs on those unable to pay off criminal justice debt immediately. For the low-income populations who make up 80 percent of criminal defendants (the percentage incapable of paying for their own defense), this additional debt becomes a further obstacle to housing and employment, which often require credit checks.[15] Criminal justice debt also acts as a de facto indicator of incarceration history, which nullifies the victories of activists across the country who have successfully "banned the box" requiring job applicants to list felony convictions.

Meanwhile the large revenue stream created by criminal justice debt creates perverse financial incentives for state and local governments to criminalize their residents. Ferguson demonstrates this dynamic in profound ways. Public safety and court fines comprised 20 percent ($2.5 million) of the municipality's total operating revenue for 2013, an 80 percent increase from 2011.[16] In 2013 alone, the city issued more than nine thousand warrants for minor violations such as parking violations. From 2011 to 2013, 95 percent of people cited in Ferguson for the essentially meaningless charges of "failure to comply" and "manner of walking in the roadway" were African American. It is under precisely this circumstance that police officer Darren Wilson fatally shot Michael Brown.[17]

While Ferguson is notorious for public predation on Black residents, it is not alone. In 2013 two smaller jurisdictions in St. Louis County, St. Ann and St. John, received an even larger portion of their revenue from fines and forfeiture—39.6 and 29.4 percent, respectively.[18] In municipalities throughout the country, fines, "user fees," and other punitive charges supply a growing source of extractive income in a time of fiscal austerity. Tellingly it is not uncommon for these charges to far exceed the costs of restitution for crime victims themselves.[19]

The private sector is also developing new ways to mine revenue from criminalized people, beyond the well-known method of for-profit prisons. Private companies now perform probation, parole, drug-rehabilitation, and reentry services on contract.[20] One of the most egregious examples is the private electronic-monitoring industry, which provides technology used for pretrial tracking of defendants, for house-arrest sentences of nonviolent offenders, and as a condition of probation. While this technology has been around since the early 1980s, the offender-funded business model originated roughly a decade later. Like SWAT teams and antigang injunctions, the earliest precedents of this for-profit model stem from Los Angeles. After the L.A. rebellion in 1992—in which law enforcement arrested more than eleven thousand people, nearly three times the total arrested in the 1965 Watts rebellion—the world's largest urban jail system was straining at the seams. Sentinel, a private company, recognized an opportunity. The company proposed that the L.A. probation department require reentering offenders to wear its monitoring system—and pay for it. Sentinel's "offender-funded justice" model promised savings for taxpayers and revenues for its shareholders. The city signed up and the contemporary era of privatized electronic monitoring began.[21]

People compelled to use the system may be charged anywhere from $9.25 to $49 per day, with monthly costs ranging between $300 and $1,519.[22] They also must pay substantial setup costs. Those who cannot pay are returned to custody, costing the monitoring companies nothing. The value of companies that provide electronic monitoring has soared as profits have rolled in. In 2011 the private-prison giant GEO Group purchased Behavioral Interventions, the country's largest electronic provider, for $415 million. It is no wonder the for-profit model of electronic monitoring has been rapidly expanding. Indeed, the bipartisan consensus on the need for decarceration has only strengthened the position of the electronic-monitoring industry.

By devolving the cost of punishment onto criminalized people themselves, the offender-funded model helps turn a profit for private firms while providing cost-savings for the municipalities that contract them. The consequences for individuals can be devastating, as in the case of Antonio Green, a disabled South Carolina resident who was arrested in 2014 for driving without a license. He initially took the option of electronic monitoring rather than jail. But after watching his financial and personal life unravel under the weight of nearly $2,500 in fees over the course of a year, Green found himself with no option but to go to jail. "I gave up," he told a reporter for *International Business Times*. "I was falling apart. It felt like being on a chain gang. Those bills were getting out of hand. I said, 'They're just going to have to lock me up.'"[23]

And so the cycle continues. Poor people face debt, jail for minor infractions, and further debt to pay for their punishment. The well of poverty grows deeper as extractive states, municipalities, and private companies seize the income of vulnerable populations.

• • •

In 1983 the Supreme Court determined, in *Bearden v. Georgia*, that a debtor could only be jailed for failing to pay a fine if it were proven that the person *could* pay the fine and willfully chose not to.[24] Drawing on the due process and equal protection clauses of the Fourteenth Amendment, the case reaffirmed earlier rulings that it is unlawful to incarcerate indigent debtors for their inability to pay—the foundation of the extractive system.

But as in the past, the law, without enforcement, has provided little remedy. History offers a lesson to today's activists: as long as there is a way for state and private entities to make money off of criminal justice, they will seek to criminalize as many people as they can. Not only did *Bearden* fail to stem the cycle of criminalization, debt, extraction, and more criminalization, but the situation has also worsened. Several factors may be at work. Chief among them is the sheer growth of the infrastructure of punishment over the last forty years, which has helped to naturalize a variety of practices that strip people of their rights and financial means. "In the 1970s and 1980s we started to imprison more people for lesser crimes," Civil Rights lawyer Alec Karakatsanis argues. "In the process, we were lowering

our standards for what constituted an offense deserving of imprisonment, and, more broadly, we were losing our sense of how serious . . .
it is to incarcerate. If we can imprison for possession of marijuana,
why can't we imprison for not paying back a loan?" Karakatsanis has
been fighting de facto debtors' prison by suing municipal courts.[25]

Another factor is the way in which many judges apply their discretionary power to determine what constitutes "willful failure" to
pay criminal justice debt. Too often judges rely on capricious and un-
predictable standards to gauge the indigence of defendants. It is not
uncommon for judges to ask whether or not defendants smoke and
decide, if the answer is yes, that they have the means to pay. Tattoos
and nice clothing have also been cited as evidence of an unwillingness to meet legal financial obligations.[26] Post-recession fiscal austerity is also driving growing extraction. Ironically, the same cutbacks
that have helped make decarceration a bipartisan initiative make
extraction that much more urgent. This is not to say that predation
disappears in times of plenty. Pervasive opposition to individual and
corporate taxes since the Reagan era has forced local jurisdictions to
supplement fiscal shortfalls, sometimes through the kind of extreme
rent-seeking behavior seen in Ferguson.

Considering the persistence, in one guise or another, of justice
system practices designed to extract capital and labor from poor
and working-class Black citizens, we need to reevaluate the history
of criminalization in America. There is a tendency to think of mass
incarceration as a relatively new phenomenon that commenced with
the War on Drugs and the political imperatives of the Nixon administration. But racially disproportionate incarceration and caging pre-
date these more recent developments. It was a necessity of slavery, of
course, but also a hallmark of Redemption and Jim Crow, when new
institutions of white domination formally replaced those outlawed by
passage of the Thirteenth, Fourteenth, and Fifteenth Amendments. It
also characterized—and continues to characterize—the policing and

confinement practices of states and municipalities throughout the North and West. Criminalization of Black, Brown, and Indigenous populations is as old as America itself and it has often been a means of predation.

Perhaps the most important lesson to be learned from the brutal history of American debt peonage and convict leasing is that many of the foundations of racial inequality are economic. Racism and white supremacy are often understood as either psychological or socially constructed ideas, thoughts, and feelings. But Jim Crow's coercive labor practices; race-based contract housing, redlining, and subprime lending; and today's cycle of debt and imprisonment remind us that the *economic* life of racism is arguably its most enduring feature. While public discourse and protocol have changed since the Civil Rights Movement—Republican president Donald Trump not withstanding—successful challenges to the deeper material inequities of racialized wealth and opportunity have proved more elusive. The foreclosure crisis triggered by the Great Recession, which impacted twice as many Black homeowners as it did white, is another reminder that racism is at its most destructive when intertwined with economic structures that facilitate profiting off the misfortunes of others.

Looking at incarceration from the point of view of debt also raises new questions about the nature of our democracy. Many people know that, in most states, those convicted of felonies lose their right to vote for a period of time—in some cases for life. Fewer realize that, in many states, a precondition for felons to regain their right to vote is that all of their criminal justice debt must first be paid.[27] This penalty functions as a modern-day poll tax, with severe consequences for the African American community in particular. Thirteen percent of African American men (nearly one in eight) cannot vote because of criminal disenfranchisement laws, about seven times the national average. Equally troubling are fees for use of public defenders, which impair low-income people's ability to receive the fair trials mandated by the

Constitution.[28] Fear of debt has led many to forego legal representation and even to plead guilty to avoid at least some financial damage.

There are, however, glimmers of hope, for example, in pushback from the Obama administration, civil libertarians, and prisoners themselves. The Ferguson protests and subsequent investigations have had an enormous impact. In March the Department of Justice's top Civil Rights prosecutor, Vanita Gupta, issued a forceful letter to state judges warning them against unconstitutional fine and jailing policies that entrap the indigent in "cycles of poverty that can be nearly impossible to escape."[29] Echoing the findings of the DOJ's March 2015 report on Ferguson's police department and court system, Gupta warned against courts adopting profit-minded policies that endanger poor people's equal access to the justice system. She also emphasized the dangers of contracting probation services to private companies that directly benefit from discretionary fines they themselves impose.[30] In early May, the Colorado ACLU also won a settlement with the city of Colorado Springs that ended the practice of jailing people for their inability to pay fines and provided compensation for those whose constitutional rights were violated.[31]

In addition to these practical reform efforts, a larger reexamination of the economic and extractive dimensions of mass incarceration is needed, apart from establishing more equitable means testing of people brought before the courts. This is especially urgent in this protean moment of decarceration in which new systems of surveillance and control, such as electronic monitoring, are being widely adopted. If justice reform relies on the offender-funded model, perverse financial incentives for greater criminalization will persist.

One of the enduring lessons from past struggle for social change is that where there is the greatest suffering, there is also the most creative and insightful response. The pattern holds in a recent compelling protest against criminalization and extraction, a May Day labor strike in an Alabama for-profit prison. "Our mass incarceration is a form of slavery, because we're not being paid for our work, but we're being charged outrageous fines," one of the prison strikers explained. Kinetik Justice, a spokesperson for the Free Alabama Movement, called for "transparency in the courts and humanity in the prison system."[32] Although the strike ended after a couple of weeks, its larger demands for prison reform, elimination of forced labor, and the end of predatory fines resonate strongly throughout the United States. Prisoners themselves—in a state with one of the most brutal histories of chain gangs and convict labor—took a stand against profiteering at their expense. Listening to their stories, and shaping policy accordingly, will help us all summon a more compassionate and just future.

CHAPTER 8

HOW RACE MADE THE OPIOID CRISIS

I n March 2018, President Donald Trump delivered a forty-minute speech about the crisis of addiction and overdose in New Hampshire. Standing before a wall tiled with the words "Opioids: The Crisis Next Door," Trump blankly recited the many contributors to the current drug epidemic, including doctors, dealers, and manufacturers. Trump droned on mechanically until he reached a venomous crescendo about Customs and Border Protection's seizure of 1,500 pounds of fentanyl. He brightened as he shifted focus to three of his most hated enemies, first blaming China and Mexico for saturating the United States with deadly synthetic opioids, then moving seamlessly to what he considered one of the great internal threats: "My administration is also confronting things called 'sanctuary cities,'" Trump declared. "Ending sanctuary cities is crucial to stopping the drug addiction crisis."[1]

Like so many of Trump's proclamations, this rhetoric is sheer political fantasy. Our ideas of drug use—which kinds are legal, and which are not—are steeped in the metalanguage of race. Since the late 1990s, yearly rates of overdose deaths from legal "white market" opioids have consistently exceeded those from heroin. According to the Centers for Disease Control and Prevention, between 1999 and 2017, opioid overdoses killed nearly four hundred thousand people with 68 percent of those deaths linked to prescription medications.[2]

---

* "How Race Made the Opioid Crisis" originally appeared in *Boston Review* (2019). Reprinted with permission.

Moreover, as regulators and drug companies tightened controls on diversion and misuse after 2010, the American Society of Addiction Medicine determined that at least 80 percent of "new heroin users started out misusing prescription pain killers." Some data sets point to even higher numbers. In response to a 2014 survey of people undergoing treatments for opioid addiction, 94 percent of people surveyed said that they turned to heroin because prescription opioids were "far more expensive and harder to obtain."[3]

In the face of these statistics, the claim that the opioid crisis is the product of Mexican and Central American migration—rather than the deregulation of Big Pharma and the failures of a private health care system—is not only absurd but also insidious. It substitutes racial myth for fact, thereby rationalizing an ever-expanding machinery of punishment while absolving one of the most lucrative, and politically influential, business lobbies in the United States. This paradoxical relationship between a racialized regime of illegal drug prohibition and a highly commercial, laissez-faire approach to prescription pharmaceuticals cannot be understood without recourse to how racial capitalism has structured pharmacological markets throughout US history. The linguistic convention of "white" and "black" markets points to how steeped our ideas of licit and illicit are in the metalanguage of race.[4]

Historically, the fundamental division between "dope" and "medicine" has been the race and class of users. The earliest salvos in the US domestic drug wars can be traced to anti-opium ordinances in late nineteenth-century California as Chinese laborers poured into the state during the railroad building boom. In 1914 the federal government passed the Harrison Narcotics Act, which taxed and regulated opiates and coca products. Similarly, as rates of immigration increased in the aftermath of the Mexican Revolution, Congress passed the Marijuana Tax Act of 1937, which targeted the customs and culture of newly settled migrants. Although "cannabis" was well known in the

United States—it was used in numerous tinctures and medicines—a racial scare campaign swept the country and warned that "marijuana" aroused men of color's violent lust for white women.[5]

As bad as the early drug panics were, they paled in comparison to the carceral regime of drug prohibition and policing that emerged in the years after the Civil Rights Movement. Starting in the early 1970s, mass incarceration and the overlapping wars on drugs and gangs increasingly displaced social policy for low-income communities of color. Legislation increased state and federal mandatory minimums for drug crime, denied public housing to entire families if any member was even suspected of a drug offense, expanded the federal death penalty, and imposed draconian restrictions of parole. As a result, multiple generations of youth of color suffered long prison sentences and faced lifelong collateral consequences.

Today, much of the Trump administration's rhetoric is taken from decades of drug and incarceration frenzies past, including the threat of the death penalty for drug trafficking (Bill Clinton), Just Say No campaigns (Ronald Reagan), and the reinvigoration of the War on Gangs (Bill Clinton again). "We are all facing a deadly lucrative international drug trade," warned Trump's then attorney general, Jeff Sessions. As he spoke before the International Association of Chiefs of Police in the fall of 2017, Sessions laid out a law-and-order platform that promised to "back the blue," reduce crime, and dismantle "transnational criminal organizations."[6] He drew so heavily from 1980s anti-drug hysteria, in fact, that he earned giddy praise from Edwin Meese III, Reagan's attorney general who helped enshrine the 100-to-1 sentencing disparity between crack and powder cocaine. "Largely unnoticed has been the extraordinary work that . . . Sessions has done in the Department of Justice to create a Reaganesque resurgence of law and order," Meese opined in *USA Today* in January 2018.[7]

From 2017 to 2018, Trump and Sessions repeatedly used the threat of drugs and racial contagion for a reactionary portfolio ranging

from reversals of modest criminal justice reforms of the Obama era—
including reinstating federal civil forfeiture, limiting federal power
to implement consent decrees at the local level, and the expansion
of mandatory minimum sentencing in the federal system—to the
building of a wall along the Mexican border. And, although anticrime
rhetoric no longer has the same purchase as it did in the era of Willie
Horton or Ricky Ray Rector—thanks in large part to activist efforts
to delegitimize mass incarceration—the reinvigorated machinery of
criminalization remains firmly in place.

Integrating the opioid crisis with the War on Drugs raises questions beyond familiar narratives and political discourses. In the United States, prohibition of illicit drugs and the mass marketing of licit
pharmaceuticals fit together in a larger framework of racial capitalism
and deregulation that are deeply intertwined and mutually reinforcing. The opioid crisis would not have been possible without the racial
regimes that have long structured both illicit and licit modes of consumption. As we will see, the demonization of urban, nonwhite drug
users played a crucial role in the opening of "white" pharmaceutical
markets in the 1990s that proved so enormously profitable to companies such as Purdue Pharma and paved the way for our current public
health crisis.[8]

In the 1990s, Purdue created aggressive marketing campaigns
to convince doctors and state regulators of the safety of a new class
of timed-release opioid analgesics. Given their status as Schedule II
controlled substances, Purdue faced potentially enormous pushback,
especially at a time when the number of people incarcerated for drug
offenses was reaching an all-time high.[9] However, a major shift had
taken place in regulatory policy a decade before that made this possible. In the 1980s, President Reagan initiated a radical program of
corporate deregulation that opened the door to a new era of pharmaceutical mass marketing. Reagan's "Second American Revolution"
slashed government oversight, pushed through expedited review by

the Food and Drug Administration (FDA), and for the first time allowed direct-to-consumer advertising for pharmaceutical drugs.[10]

Amazingly, the deregulation of Big Pharma took place while the Reagan administration was launching a bombastic Second War on Drugs that established a new standard for illicit drug prohibition, one his successors George H. W. Bush and Bill Clinton not only met but exceeded. This potent mix of racialized drug prosecution and corporate empowerment created the environment in which Purdue and other companies sought out new commercial strategies for marketing opioids.

So, when Purdue introduced OxyContin in 1996, it proceeded with an awareness of both the opportunities and potential pitfalls. The company developed a number of marketing strategies to increase sales *and* to navigate the deeply segregated waters of drug consumption. In order to market OxyContin, a long-term release opioid that contains the active ingredient oxycodone, Purdue created an expansive network of sales representatives, doubling its internal sales force from 318 in 1996 to 671 in 2000.[11] Driven by sophisticated data collection methods that revealed the highest and lowest prescribers in every zip code throughout the United States, Purdue identified medical practices with the largest numbers of pain patients and with physicians who were the least discriminate prescribers.[12] Sales representatives received bonuses ranging from $15,000 to $240,000 a year for increases in opioid prescriptions in their coverage areas, and they visited doctors repeatedly, drawing them into an elaborate informational marketing campaign. Purdue offered doctors educational conferences in Sunbelt resorts, patient coupons, OxyContin-branded stuffed animals, and even CDs of the drug's marketing jingle, "Get in the Swing of OxyContin."

The company's aggressive sales tactics convinced primary care physicians (PCPs) to prescribe opioids much more frequently for a wide range of patient complaints, including lower back pain and arthritis. By 2003 PCPs made up nearly half of OxyContin prescribers. Some experts at the time worried that PCPs lacked independent training in chronic pain management and addiction.[13] Meanwhile the increase in the sale of OxyContin—from $48 million upon its introduction to $1.1 billion four years later—demonstrates the enormous scale of this enterprise.[14]

According to public health scholars Helena Hansen and Julie Netherland, Purdue's success hinged not only on this aggressive sales campaign, but also on racially bifurcated understandings of addiction. Drug sales representatives directed advertisement to overwhelmingly white suburban and rural areas to avoid the stigma of racially coded urban drug markets. By crafting a geographically distinct, white consumer base—understood as the antithesis of "hardcore" (nonwhite) urban drug users targeted by the wars on drugs and gangs—the company both benefited from and reinforced the racial ideology underwriting these punitive campaigns.

Not surprisingly, the regions that initially showed the highest rates of opioid abuse in the early 2000s—including rural Maine, West Virginia, Kentucky, and western Pennsylvania—had overwhelmingly white populations. Although the press termed OxyContin "hillbilly heroin" and the drug of choice for poor whites, public health researchers have shown that affluent suburbanites also had high rates of abuse, exemplified by Rush Limbaugh's disclosure of his own prescription opioid abuse in 2003.[15] Racial disparities in health care access, discriminatory prescribing patterns among physicians, and a self-conscious strategy by pharmaceutical companies that cultivated "legitimate" white consumer markets all contributed to the racial demographics of the opioid crisis.

A key reason that pharmaceutical companies could market such a powerful sustained-release analgesic to treat "non-malignant pain" was that they made assumptions about their intended consumers. "The disproportionate uptake of OxyContin by rural and suburban prescribers in majority white states (Maine, Kentucky and West Virginia) is notable in light of the historical hostility of regulatory agencies such as the DEA to the expansion of opioid use," argue Hansen and Netherland. "Urban markets would have brought with them race and class imagery of illicit use that may have made expanded prescription of OxyContin for moderate pain a hard sell to regulators."[16]

In a similar line of analysis, pharmaceutical historian David Herzberg, author of *Happy Pills in America: From Miltown to Prozac*, places the opioid crisis in the larger sweep of US history. According to Herzberg, there is no real difference between prescription medicines and illicit drugs. Both possess physical and psychoactive effects, but the social meaning attributed to them has more to do with race, class, and differential application of state power than pharmacology. The contemporary disparity between licit and illicit has its origins in the Jim Crow era, when the Supreme Court established the principle of separate but equal.[17] In the years after World War II, the Civil Rights Movement challenged racial discrimination in consumer markets, rendering illegal the most overt forms of discrimination, such as segregated lunch counters, public conveyances, and housing covenants. But the racialized division between licit and illicit drug markets endured. Indeed, it provided a primary rationale for the wars on drugs and crime that emerged after the Voting Rights Act. Today African Americans and Latinos make up 80 percent of those incarcerated in federal prisons for drug crimes and 60 percent of those in state prisons.[18]

One of the most compelling aspects of Herzberg's analysis is his historical exploration of how postwar white consumers defined themselves against racially coded, urban drug users by redefining pharmacological relief as an entitlement. In the same period that Richard Nixon launched the first War on Drugs, white consumers steeped in the discourse of the silent majority demanded access to pharmaceuticals as a citizenship right.[19] "I, as one American citizen make demand at this writing to restore all the drugs that people need," argued a complaint to the FDA. "Too many people are suffering and being penalized on account of the drug abusers."[20]

This "problematic social entitlement" functioned as the flip side of the more familiar story of criminalization and divestment of Black and Brown populations in the wars on drugs and crime. Prohibition of urban vice required a space of white absolution that enabled the profitable mass-marketing of licit pharmaceuticals. "A focus on pharmaceutical white markets tells a very different story: of a divided system of drug control designed to encourage and enable a segregated market for psychoactive substances," Herzberg argues. "This regime established a privilege—maximal freedom of rational choice in a relatively safe drug market . . . and linked this privilege both institutionally and culturally to social factors such as economic class and whiteness."[21]

Cultural logics, as well as criminal justice policy, have also reinforced and animated the racialized boundary between "licit health seekers" and "illicit pleasure seekers" in the popular imagination.[22] Iconic drug films such as *Traffic* (2000) and *Requiem for a Dream* (2000) dramatize the tragedy of white women's descent into illegal narcotic use through pornographic narratives in which "innocent" young white girls are coerced into interracial sex by Black male "pushers." Drawing on the cinematic grammar of D. W. Griffith's classic KKK paean *Birth of a Nation* (1915), they reenact the white supremacist ideology that reinforced racial segregation. Viewed in this way, the opioid crisis appears not as an unprecedented phenomenon, but the product of long-standing historical processes.

The role of white absolution is even clearer when looking at the disparate consequences for illicit drug use across the color line. Nothing speaks more profoundly to how the state artificially constructed segregated drug markets than federal prosecutions for crack use. Few realize that almost no white people were ever charged with crack offenses by federal authorities. This is despite the federal government's

own data from the National Institute of Drug Abuse (NIDA) documenting that over two-thirds of crack users were white. Between 1986,
when Congress signed the Anti-Drug Abuse Act into law, and 1994,
when President Clinton's crime bill was passed, not a single white person was convicted of a federal crack offense in Miami, Boston, Denver,
Chicago, Dallas, or Los Angeles. "Out of hundreds of cases, only one
white was convicted in California, two in Texas, three in New York and
two in Pennsylvania," noted *Los Angeles Times* reporter Dan Weikel.[23]
Instead, prosecutors shunted their cases into the state system, which
had much lower rates of conviction and shorter sentences.

At the heart of this disparity is the paradoxical relationship in the
United States between prohibition and provision: some of the harsh-
est advocates for punishment and the criminalization of illicit drug
use have also enthusiastically supported and defended pharmaceutical deregulation and expanded access to opioids. If there is any doubt
about Trump's acquiescence to Big Pharma—despite his campaign
promises to lower Medicare drug prices—one need look no further
than his appointment of Alex Azar II, former president of the US division of pharmaceutical giant Eli Lilly and Co., to serve as secretary
of health and human services.[24]

The career of Rudolph Giuliani is one of the best examples of this
cognitive dissonance around drug policy that can only properly be
understood as a product of racial capitalism. As mayor of New York
(1994–2001), Giuliani and his police commissioner, William Bratton,
were central architects of the city's zero-tolerance, quality-of-life policing, which criminalized low-level offenses ranging from panhandling
and graffiti to illegal vending and minor cannabis possession. Giuliani's
administration presided over about forty thousand marijuana arrests
per year, up nearly fortyfold from the Dinkins years.[25] In fact, the highest number of marijuana possession arrests ever recorded in New York
City took place under the Giuliani administration, with 51,267 arrests
in the year 2000.[26] Giuliani also led a vicious campaign against meth-

adone treatment in the 1990s, advocating complete abstinence as the only acceptable response to illicit drugs.[27]

Given his hard-line stance on drug prohibition, it is striking that two years after New York's all-time high for marijuana arrests, the former New York mayor and prosecutor took on Purdue Pharma as a client, agreeing to help the company fend off a federal investigation into improper marketing of OxyContin. "There are tens of millions of Americans suffering from persistent pain," argued Giuliani. "We must find a way to ensure access to appropriate prescription pain medications for those suffering from the debilitating effects of pain while working to prevent the abuse and diversion of these same vital medicines."[28]

John Brownlee, a US attorney from the Western District of Virginia, initiated the investigation into Purdue Pharma shortly after his federal appointment in response to skyrocketing numbers of opioid overdoses in his region. "This was pushed by the company to be marketed in an illegal way, pushed from the highest levels of the company, that in my view made them a criminal enterprise that needed to be dealt with," Brownlee explained. Although the young attorney's legal action was the first successful criminal suit against Purdue, the company currently faces a number of civil suits from other states, including Texas, New York, Indiana, and Massachusetts. (Already, in March, it agreed to a $270 million settlement with the state of Oklahoma.)[29] In the Virginia case, Giuliani provided Purdue with legal services as well as access to his extensive network of political connections in Washington. He finessed an agreement that kept senior executives from serving prison time and attempted to restrict future prosecution of Purdue.[30]

According to the *Guardian*, Giuliani's intervention avoided "a bar on Purdue doing business with the federal government which would have killed a large part of the multibillion-dollar market for the drug."[31] Activists, investigative journalists, and public sector attorneys have produced a significant body of work documenting the culpability of pharmaceutical companies in the contemporary opioid crisis.[32] Until quite recently, however, this history has largely failed to penetrate mainstream opinion.[33] Despite the pathbreaking investigative journalism of Barry Meier's *Pain Killer* (2003) and Chris McGreal's *American Overdose* (2018), popular exposés have frequently centered on unethical practices by individual doctors and "pill mills," rather than excavating how Purdue and other companies built a commercial infrastructure that revolutionized narcotics sale at enormous social cost. Culpability is shared by a resource-starved FDA and regulatory infrastructure's failure to intervene when it became apparent that widespread abuse was taking place. Unfortunately, the young have been the hardest hit. The *New York Times* recently estimated that in 2018 nearly four hundred thousand people who were addicted to prescription opioids or heroin were between eighteen and twenty-five years old. Even more troubling is that in states such as Ohio and West Virginia with the highest rates of prescription opioid consumption, 50–80 percent of foster care placements were linked to substance abuse in the home.[34] In the realm of health and human pain, free market fundamentalism has proved quite deadly.

The origins of the opioid crisis in the licit pharmaceutical market calls not only for a rethinking of the politics of deregulation, but also an end to the sclerotic, racialized War on Drugs narrative still mobilized by the Trump administration. In moving testimony before the House Judiciary Committee on Immigration and Border Security, Stanford psychologist and West Virginia native Keith Humphreys spoke directly to this issue in February 2018:

> West Virginia is emblematic of where this epidemic is at its most destructive—rural areas that don't have sanctuary cities and indeed generally don't have cities at all. Recent immigrants are rare, yet opioid addiction is rampant. That's because the opioid epidemic was made in America, not in Mexico, China, or any other

foreign country. The astonishing increase in providing opioids—
which at its apex reached nearly a quarter billion prescriptions
per year—is what started and still maintains our opioid epidemic.
Prescription opioids come from American companies and are pre-
scribed by American doctors overseen by American regulators.[35]

Like many crises, our current dilemma also presents opportunities to radically rethink our approaches to both prohibition and
provision. In addition to recognizing the role of Big Pharma, a critical look at the opioid crisis also requires examining the larger environment in which this predatory marketing campaign took place.
Structural issues of economic downward mobility, diminished occupational safety and health protections, lack of health care access, and
the limitations of managed care have all contributed.

Critically, we must push back against the racist logic that has long
underwritten prohibition efforts while occluding, and even assisting,
the pharmaceutical industry's attempt to expand its reach. Phantasms
of drug sale and consumption continue to animate deeply felt national narratives demarcating the line between white and Black, native
and foreign, innocent and guilty, medical and recreational, deserving
and undeserving, licit and illicit. The Trump administration, like its
Democratic and Republican predecessors, drew some of its most destructive symbols of racial animus from the War on Drugs' repertoire.
One of the most important lessons to be learned from viewing the
opioid crisis and the drug war through the lens of racial capitalism is
that the privileges of whiteness come at a great social cost not only
for those excluded from them but also for those who possess them.
As our nation witnesses a significant drop in life expectancy due to
high rates of suicide and overdose, an honest reckoning with the true
nature of power and culpability in the United States has never been
more urgent.

CHAPTER 9

The Movement for Black Lives

A Retrospective Look from 2021

The morning after four Minneapolis police officers suffocated George Floyd, a forty-six-year-old Black resident and father of five, the United States entered the most sustained period of civil unrest in its history. Video footage from bystanders showed an excruciating scene with officer Derek Chauvin pressing his knee into Floyd's neck, as the handcuffed man begged for his life, telling officers over a dozen times, "I can't breathe." After nearly eight minutes in this position, Floyd cried out for his deceased mother and lost consciousness. He was later pronounced dead in a local hospital after suffering cardiac arrest. His alleged crime was purchasing a packet of cigarettes with a $20 counterfeit bill. Like the shootings of Minneapolis residents Jamar Clark and Philando Castile and the more than five thousand people killed by law enforcement since Michael Brown's death by police in Ferguson, Missouri, this kind of everyday, racial violence was routine. Historian Elizabeth Hinton described the killing as "a devastating incident of state violence with deep historical roots."[1]

In the days to come, mass civil disobedience swept through the city of Minneapolis as thousands of people filled the streets, with much of their ire focused on the Third Street police precinct. Residual anger over the police killing of twenty-six-year-old Breonna Taylor in Kentucky two and a half months before Floyd's death also informed the spread of the protest. Armed with a "no-knock" warrant, officers from the Louisville Police Department shot the young emergency room technician at least eight times, killing her in her own home.[2] Within forty-eight hours of Floyd's death, authorities still had not charged Chauvin and the other three officers, despite flagrant violations of protocol. Instead, local law enforcement responded with aggressive crowd control tactics, tear gas, and rubber bullets that quickly escalated the scale and tenor of the protest. Most daytime demonstrations remained peaceful; however, a contingent of protestors targeted symbols of police power with rocks, bottles, and Molotov cocktails. Attacks on property spilled out to the surrounding area as residents seized goods from retail shops like Target and AutoZone to set them ablaze. By May 29th, the city of Minneapolis's third precinct was burned to the ground as multiracial crowds of demonstrators expressed fury not only about Floyd, but also about systemic police abuse, economic marginalization, and the devastating effects of COVID-19 on populations of color. In the Minneapolis metro area, Black and American Indian residents' poverty rates exceeded those of white residents more than fivefold.[3]

The sheer size and scale of uprisings for Black Lives that ensued from May 26, 2020, through the end of the summer in 2020 dwarfed any previous period of social unrest in American history. In order to understand how this critical inflection point was reached, this essay limns the organizational and intellectual foundations of the Black Lives Matter Movement over the past decade. Drawing its inspiration from Black Feminist theory and praxis, and its iconography from Black Panther and Black Liberation Army member Assata Shakur, a younger generation of millennial activists built a capacious movement challenging the structures of racialized criminalization, dispossession, and anti-Black violence in the United States. Uprisings in Minneapolis inspired solidarity efforts that have quickly spread throughout the United States as calls for the abolition and defunding of police entered the mainstream media. The events in

Minneapolis quickly ignited demonstrations throughout the US and other parts of the world. By the first week in July, between 15 and 26 million Americans took to the streets in mass demonstrations throughout the country with a little less than half of all counties in the US taking part. This was no small feat. As the other essays in this volume demonstrate, until very recently, mounting a sustained, popular opposition to racialized incarceration and the politics of divestment, extraction, and racial capitalism that underwrite it has proved very difficult. Over the past decade, however, a younger generation of Black activists, drawing on the rich political culture of queer and nonbinary organizing, have created a social movement that simultaneously confronts state violence while also challenging gendered and patriarchal forms of power.

TRAYVON MARTIN AND THE CYBERNETIC POLITICS OF BLACK DEATH

On February 26, 2012, Trayvon Martin, a seventeen-year-old boy with a slight build and easy smile, left his father's fiancée's gated residential community in Sanford, Florida, to purchase Skittles and Arizona Iced Tea from a local 7-Eleven convenience store. That night, Martin happened to be wearing khaki slacks cuffed at the ankle and a hooded sweatshirt, a detail that would be entirely unremarkable were it not for the racial meta-narratives brought to bear in the months to come. On the way back from the store, George Zimmerman, a twenty-eight-year-old insurance underwriter, who had a history of reporting Black boys as young as seven to the police, began stalking Martin with a 9mm handgun. Local authorities knew Zimmerman well; he had repeatedly called 911 as a self-appointed neighborhood watchman. He also had a record as a criminal defendant that included a school suspension for marijuana possession, an arrest in 2005 for battery of a policeman, and a 2007 complaint of battery from a former girlfriend. By contrast, Trayvon Martin had no history of priors.[4]

Zimmerman's own racial status was somewhat ambiguous: he identi-fied as Hispanic on census forms, as his mother was born in Peru, his father a white native-born former Army sergeant.[5]

Empowered by Florida's Stand Your Ground (SYG) laws, Zim-merman took it upon himself to track people he viewed as potential intruders to the majority-white housing development.[6] This section of Florida's criminal statute on the use of deadly force and home de-fense states, "A person who is not engaged in an unlawful activity and who is *attacked in any other place where he or she has a right to be* has no duty to retreat and has the right to stand his or her ground and meet force with force, including deadly force if he or she reasonably believes it is necessary to do so to prevent death or bodily harm to himself or herself or another or to prevent the commission of a forc-ible felony."[7] Drawing on an older set of English common law statutes known as the Castle Doctrine, the SYG laws expanded the param-eters of self defense in key ways beyond the actual protection of one's home to one's physical self, and in certain states, one's personal property items such as wallets or automobiles. Ultimately, the law ex-panded the right to use deadly force to "any other place where he or she has a right to be." Shortly after calling the police, Zimmerman confronted Martin, and shot him in the chest and killed him. While Zimmerman never directly invoked the SYG law in his defense, his entire case and actions that evening drew upon its suppositions.

Seven years before the murder of Trayvon Martin, the state of Florida adopted the first explicit SYG law in 2005 with an overwhelm-ing vote of support in the state house of 94 to 20. The following year, nearly a dozen states adopted similar statutes, and by 2011, just one year before Martin's brutal slaying, the number had nearly doubled. Led by the conservative lobbying group the American Legislative Ex-change Council (ALEC) and the National Rifle Association (NRA), SYG laws spread rapidly through adjacent states Georgia, Alabama, Mississippi, and Louisiana up through the Republican strongholds

of Kentucky, Oklahoma, Kansas, South Dakota, and northern Wisconsin, before blanketing much of the remaining red expanse of the
South, West, and Midwest. This pattern was an important one because
it showed Zimmerman's individual exercise of violence was tied to a
larger pattern of policy and practices that underwrote state and private
racial violence. Indeed, as scholar Beth Richie and others have argued,
in practical terms, the two are inseparable from one another.[8]

In this context, Trayvon Martin emerged as the iconic symbol of a
burgeoning Movement for Black Lives nearly a decade before the killings
of Breonna Taylor and George Floyd. The fallen seventeen-year-old—
memorialized by the hoodie itself—came to personify the vulnerability
of the Black body in the era of America's first Black president. It is notable that Martin hailed from the state that, over a century before, had the
highest per capita rate of lynching in the Jim Crow South. Its campaign
of terror and dispossession was a direct response to Florida's large percentage of nineteenth-century Black property ownership and a resilient
Black Republican party that refused to capitulate to the Compromise
of 1877.[9] The history of Martin's home state reminds us that the fabric
of contemporary state-sanctioned racial violence is taken whole cloth
from American history, from antebellum slave patrols, spectacle lynching, convict leasing, immigration and border policing, and, of course,
the genocide of Native peoples.

Social media played a crucial role in transforming Martin's brutal
slaying into a cause célèbre that catalyzed Black youth protest. As the
mainstream media cannibalized its most popular content, social media
brought material into view that otherwise would have been overlooked
or ignored. The importance of digital media to the Movement for Black
Lives first became visible on a large scale after BART Officer Johannes
Mehserle's shooting of Oscar Grant as he lay facedown and immobi-
lized on a train platform on New Year's Day 2009. Similarly, during the
massive campaign to prevent the death row execution of Troy Davis in
2011, Facebook memes and Twitter hashtags became crucial ways to

create a national platform of support. Black Twitter became a force of reckoning, but few understood why. Contrary to the dire predictions of a yawning racial digital divide of the 1990s, African Americans emerged as a disproportionate virtual presence. A 2013 report from the Pew Research Center noted that 40 percent of Black youth ages 18–29 used Twitter in comparison to 28 percent of whites. While it would be a mistake to understand the grassroots movement against racial violence as a reflexive technological creation—similarly overly deterministic claims were made about the Arab uprisings from Tunisia to Tahrir Square— digital platforms did make it possible to publicize the killings of Black people ignored by the corporate press. Police violence that had only received coverage through the carceral lens of crime reporting now became a site for political mobilization as activists called attention to the onslaught of Black death.[10]

BLACK LIVES MATTER—HASHTAG, POLITICAL IDEOLOGY, OR NETWORK

Most observers of what has come to be known as the Black Lives Matter Movement trace its origins back to Trayvon Martin's murder and George Zimmerman's acquittal, which came in July of 2013. The simultaneous mobilization of Black youth across the country, knitted together through bonds of social media, represented a "borning" moment, to use Bernice J. Reagon's term, that engendered the Black Lives Matter hashtag and subsequent political network, as well as Florida-based Dream Defenders, Black Youth Project 100, and mass street protests that coalesced into what many at the time referred to as "the anti-state sanctioned violence movement."[11] This rather cumbersome term has since been replaced by the more precise phrase, the Movement for Black Lives.[12]

In a story that has become political legend, the founders of Black Lives Matter coined the phrase that journeyed from hashtag to political network, and ultimately, to an expansive umbrella term for

Black youth protest of the early twenty-first century. In July 2013, during the disorienting aftermath of George Zimmerman's acquittal in which his defense team tried Trayvon Martin posthumously by accusing him of drug use and thuggery, Alicia Garza posted a powerful impromptu commentary on Facebook: "The sad part is, there's a section of America who is cheering and celebrating right now. and that makes me sick to my stomach. We GOTTA get it together y'all." She went on, "stop saying we are not surprised. that's a damn shame in itself. I continue to be surprised at how little Black lives matter. And I will continue that. stop giving up on Black life." Garza concluded, "Black people I love you. I love us. Our lives matter."[13]

Fellow Los Angeles organizer Patrisse Cullors recognized the transcendent phrasing and shortened Garza's post into a Twitter hashtag: "#BlackLivesMatter." Soon, Garza and Cullors reached out to Opal Tometi, who set up Twitter and Tumblr accounts under the new phrase, whose use steadily grew over the next years, peaking in the aftermath of the Ferguson street protests. While the collaborative hashtag activism of #BlackLivesMatter quickly went viral, it mattered that Garza, Cullors, and Tometi all had extensive experience in the world of political organizing and progressive not-for-profits, and had substantial social media followings. In 2012, Garza worked as the executive director of People Organized to Win Employment Rights (POWER) before assuming a position as special project coordinator for the Oakland office of the National Domestic Workers Alliance. Patrisse Cullors headed up Dignity and Power Now, a small not-for-profit group advocating reform of the Los Angeles County Sheriff's Department. And in New York, long-term organizer Opal Tometi served as the executive director of Black Alliance for Just Immigration, which focused on migrant populations of African descent. Both Cullors and Garza identified as queer, and had done LGBTQ organizing in the past.[14]

In October 2014, two years after the founding of the Black Lives Matter hashtag, Alicia Garza described their shared political vision:

Black Lives Matter is a unique contribution that goes beyond extrajudicial killings of Black people by police and vigilantes. It goes beyond the narrow nationalism that can be prevalent within some Black communities, which merely call on Black people to love Black, live Black and buy Black, keeping straight cis Black men in the front of the movement while our sisters, queer and trans and disabled folk take up roles in the background or not at all. Black Lives Matter affirms the lives of Black queer and trans folks, disabled folks, Black-undocumented folks, folks with records, women and all Black lives along the gender spectrum. It centers those that have been marginalized within Black liberation movements. It is a tactic to (re) build the Black liberation movement.[15]

Initially, Black Lives Matter was only thought of as a hashtag, but as the corporate media increasingly reported all forms of Black protest as Black Lives Matter, the line between the many different regional and ideological tendencies became blurred. Participants varied from the tight-knit structure of BYP100 to the mass spontaneous demonstrations in Ferguson, Missouri; Baltimore, Maryland; Charlotte, North Carolina; Oakland, California; and many other locales. While the mainstream press often reported these many and varied actions as Black Lives Matter protest, in truth they represented distinct tendencies, with different social and geographical profiles.

Washington Post journalist Wesley Lowery, who did extensive on-the-ground coverage of the Ferguson protests during its first few months, argues that in its earliest iteration, Black Lives Matter was best understood as a set of ideas rather than as a full-fledged social movement. "For the young Black men and women entering the adult world during the Obama presidency, the ideology of Black Lives Matter, not yet an organization nor a movement, carried substance, even heft," argued Lowery. "It was a message that resonated with the young Black men and women who had been so outraged and pained by the Zimmerman verdict. And the decision by Tometi to focus on Twitter and Tumblr, then second-tier social media outlets, instead of

Facebook, proved a stroke of strategic genius."[16] BLM asserted that anti-Blackness represented the original sin of American life and history upon which all other forms of inequality were built, therefore, in the words of the Combahee River Collective, "when Black people get free, everybody gets free."[17] Viewed in this way, the campaign against state violence represented a larger struggle against all forms of oppression. Initially, activists faced the challenge of translating this new conceptual framework into a national organizing project with a concrete political agenda and policy objectives.

Patrisse Cullors's confrontation with Bernie Sanders at the Netroots conference in the spring of 2015 also raised the question of the extent to which the Black Lives Matter Global Network (BLMGN), or its cofounders, would directly engage electoral politics. In its earliest iteration, the network eschewed any partisan affiliation and maintained its independence from the two-party system. By the summer of 2015, however, sustained uprisings and organization deepened with a convening in Cleveland that brought together more than a thousand participants from across the country to organize a new kind of formation. Under the umbrella of the Movement for Black Lives, a broad range of local activists, political organizers, nonprofit staff, academics, formerly incarcerated people, and newly politicized youth came together to begin the hard work of grassroots social change, building coalitions among Black organizations and creating a concrete agenda for radical transformation.[18]

Central to the shared ideology that brought together a variety of groups and tendencies under the rubric of BLMM/M4BL was the insistence that race-based analysis of state violence remained incomplete if it did not address inequities on the basis of gender or sexuality. Accordingly, private violence against women and LGBTQ populations proved essential to Black Liberation and could not be artificially separated from the struggle against state violence, police killings, and incarceration. Consistently, young activists articulated a link between "anti-Black racism" and "heteropatriarchy."[19] The BLM founders also expressed a strong concern about the potential appropriation of their hashtag along with the thoughts, efforts, and knowledge production of its participants. "When you adopt the work of queer women of color, don't name or recognize it, and promote it as if it has no history of its own; such actions are problematic," argued Alicia Garza in a 2014 piece for the *Feminist Wire*. The uncomfortable tension between building a larger movement and claiming intellectual property has persisted throughout BLM's trajectory as both a hashtag and as a political network.[20]

THE DREAM DEFENDERS AND THE BLACK RADICAL TRADITION OF MULTIRACIAL ORGANIZING

Although Black Lives Matter emerged as a national lens for Black youth revolt and organizing, it actually reflected, and sometimes obscured, the regional development of grassroots tendencies across the country. Some of these groups like Florida's Dream Defenders predated the Black Lives Matter hashtag. Along with the panoply of new activist organizations that cropped up across the US between 2012 and 2016, the Dream Defenders reflected the realities of local communities of color and the university campus culture where they formed. While the corporate media branded varied types of political organizing and expression generically as "Black Lives Matter" protest, in reality, there was a broad diversity of thought, politics, and organizing method.

The founding of the Florida-based Dream Defenders emerged in the long shadow cast by Trayvon Martin's murder, and it soon became one of the foundational tendencies in BLMM/M4BL. Its antecedents lay in student-led protest over the 2006 death of Martin Lee Anderson. Nearly a decade before, officials had sentenced the fourteen-year-old Black youth to Bay County Boot Camp, a state-run juvenile detention center in Panama City, Florida, for going joyriding in his grandmother's car. Anderson suffered a brutal death after boot camp personnel coerced him into a daily one-mile run, and when Anderson faltered, seven guards held him down, covered his face, and forced him to inhale ammonia as a nurse looked on impassively. Although an initial autopsy attributed his death to his genetic sickle-cell trait, a subsequent autopsy by an appointee of Governor Jeb Bush identified suffocation as the cause of death.[21]

Local high school students and collegians from three Tallahassee schools—Florida A&M University (the country's third largest Historically Black University), Tallahassee Community College, and Florida State University—rallied around his case and organized a sustained campaign along with members of the Anderson family. Strikingly, a year after the passage of the Stand Your Ground laws, and six years before Zimmerman murdered Trayvon Martin, youth of color in Florida took to the streets to protest state violence against their peers. Activists' efforts forced the state of Florida to shut down all five of its boot camp detention centers, to tender the resignation of its "top cop" Guy Tunnell, who headed up Florida's Department of Law Enforcement. They also insisted that the state prosecute the seven guards and the nurse involved in the fatal assault on Anderson. Although a jury trial acquitted the guards, one of the future founders of the Dream Defenders, Philip Agnew, remembered how Anderson's killing politicized him. The case starkly illustrated the fragility of Black life and how political protest and organizing could have far-reaching effects. "That transformed my whole view on life," Agnew recalled. "To see somebody as young as fourteen years old die in the care of people that were supposed to protect and serve him, as well as to rehabilitate him, seriously struck me, so I got involved."[22]

In March 2012, after the murder of Trayvon Martin, dozens of Florida activists came together, including Agnew, Vanessa Baden, and other seasoned youth organizers from the Anderson case. They created a new organization that linked the living memory of Martin Luther King Jr.'s 1963 "I Have a Dream" speech to the contemporary realities of South Florida's Black and Brown communities. From its start, the group was overwhelmingly Black-led, yet multiracial in composition. Phillip Agnew, who subsequently changed his name to Umi Selah, cofounded the Dream Defenders with Ahmad Nabil Abuznaid, a Palestinian émigré from East Jerusalem who had grown up under the Israeli occupation. A larger group of young activists was involved in the group's founding, including charter members Ciara Taylor, Nailah Summers, and Nelini Stamp, an Afro-Caribbean activist who helped organize New York's original Occupy Wall Street encampment. Eschewing a tradition of individualized charismatic leadership, the Dream Defenders considered everyone who participated in their inaugural march from Daytona to Sanford, Florida, to be cofounders.[23]

The history of the Dream Defenders demonstrates the complex interplay of ground-level direct action protest and social media that catalyzed the Movement for Black Lives. From its inception, the Dream Defenders proved particularly effective at mobilizing people and garnering press attention. Indeed, they played a crucial role in turning Trayvon Martin's killing into a national story. In April 2012, the Defenders sponsored a three-day, forty-mile march from Bethune-Cookman University in Daytona to Sanford that drew directly on the Civil Rights Movement tradition of nonviolent civil disobedience. The marchers slept in African Methodist Episcopal churches and connected with local people along the protest route. Similarly, a year later, after a jury with eleven white members acquitted George Zimmerman of second-degree murder, the Defenders occupied the state capitol for thirty-one days. This action garnered extensive national press and helped transform Martin's killing into a cause célèbre that mobilized new activist groups across the country, thereby projecting the slain seventeen-year-old's name into the national consciousness. A similar interplay between live protest and social media emerged during the popular uprising in Ferguson, Missouri, after police shot Michael Brown and left him to die in the street, as the world watched via the mediums of Facebook, Twitter, and Instagram.[24]

In contrast to some of its peer organizations, the Dream Defenders incorporated a more explicit anti-capitalist program that stressed the importance of Black and Brown alliances. In part, their decision to identify as a Black-led revolutionary organization with smaller numbers of Latinos and working-class whites reflected the realities of race and ethnicity in South Florida. Large portions of the population hailed from the Spanish-speaking and Anglophone Caribbean, Latin America, and other parts of the globe. In this coastal region of the US, separating Black and Brown populations is difficult if not impossible, as language, nation, color, and origin mingle in innumerable ways. The sheer heterodoxy of African descent populations from Haiti, Puerto Rico, Jamaica, the American South, Cuba, and numerous nations spread throughout the Caribbean basin and Latin America, combined with overlapping political traditions of the Haitian Revolution and the American Civil Rights Movement, necessitated a broad and flexible approach to Black politics. One member explained, "Part of that is being in Florida. What is Blackness in South Florida when so many people are from all the islands? [We] are inspired by the Haitian Revolution [in which] Blackness was a political identity. . . . The Black radical tradition of multiracial organizing has always been a part of our kind of ethos."[25]

Like the Vision for Black Lives mission to which they contributed, the Dream Defenders' website announces a set of beliefs and demands harkening back to the Black Panther Party's Ten-Point Program. It outlines an explicitly anti-capitalist, feminist program that embraces all forms of community self-defense and opposition to imperialism:

◊   We believe that our liberation necessitates the destruction
    of the political and economic systems of Capitalism and
    Imperialism as well as Patriarchy.
◊   We believe in People over profits.
◊   We believe that nonviolent resistance is "the only morally
    and practically sound method open to oppressed people in
    their struggle for freedom" and are fundamentally committed
    to nonviolence as our means of struggle against a violent
    oppressor.
◊   We want an immediate end to the police state and murder
    of Black people, other people of color, and other oppressed
    peoples in the United States, the immediate release of the
    2.5 million prisoners of the United States' War on the Poor,
    and trials by juries of our peers.
◊   We want an immediate end to all wars of aggression (do-
    mestic and abroad).
◊   We want a democracy that is fair and protects the right to
    vote for all.
◊   We want free, fully-funded public education for all that teach-
    es us our true history and our role in present-day society.
◊   We want community control of land, bread, housing, edu-
    cation, justice, peace, and technology.
◊   We want more. We deserve more. We will organize, train,
    act, and win.[26]

While remaining firmly committed to the inclusive united front
of the Movement for Black Lives, the Dream Defenders maintained
their own distinct vision of Black radical politics. One of the core
organizing principles of contemporary BLM protest was its emphasis on Black-only spaces and political groups. By contrast, the
Dream Defenders created a Black-led, multiracial organization rather
than limiting the participation of Latinx populations, working-class

whites, and other vulnerable populations to the status of allies or co-conspirators.

Another arena in which the Florida-based group charted its own unique course was its approach to the digital world. From its inception, the Dream Defenders, like their peer organizations, used social media platforms to great effect. By 2014, they had more than twenty-seven thousand Twitter followers, and had set up an innovative artwork display by its members called "Blacked Out History" on Tumblr. However, as the Dream Defenders evolved and assessed their priorities, they became disillusioned with social media as the primary platform for debate and outreach for the burgeoning movement. During the fall of 2015, they staged a three-month-long social media Blackout, in which they shut down all of their digital platforms, including Facebook, Twitter, Instagram, and Tumblr. "The answer is clear for us: Social media is a microphone—it amplifies the grassroots organizing work that we are doing to transform our circumstances. It does not, and never will, take the place of building deep relationships which are at the core of organizing," read the announcement of the social media boycott on September 21, 2015. "Everything outside of that—though important in shifting culture, changing policy, and transforming our communities—simply is not organizing. To change our communities, we must have power, not just followers."[27]

Finally, and perhaps most significantly, the Dream Defenders articulated a forceful critique of the not-for-profit fundraising model that supported the majority of social justice groups in the US. Although they used the tax filing status of a 501(c)(3) as a practical matter, many members felt that the "NGOization of the Dream Defenders" posed particular obstacles for building a true grassroots movement that was accountable to its base rather than philanthropic foundations or the mainstream media. "We don't identify as a nonprofit," argued strategy director Rachel Gilmer. "We identify as a revolutionary organization that has not-for-profit status." Raising external funding forced the president to travel frequently, thereby undermining trust and creating distance with the rank-and-file membership. Moreover, the NGO model exacerbated divisions between paid and unpaid organizers at a time when many millennials faced bleak job prospects. It did not always seem fair that some activists received compensation, while others had to search for ways to survive, sometimes working for other not-for-profits that did not align with their political convictions.

Outside factors also played a role in their search for alternate funding sources. The Dream Defenders' strong support for "Free Palestine" and the Boycott, Divestment, and Sanctions movement alienated a significant portion of their donor base. Ultimately, reasons both internal and external led the organization to question whether its earlier model was viable. In response, the Dream Defenders experimented with new methods to generate revenue. They started their own sweat-shop-free apparel cooperative called Rebel Threads, and staff established a membership dues structure combined with individual small-donor campaigns. The Trump years hastened this new approach to fundraising, as many feared that the far-right-wing drift of the federal government would lead to the Dream Defenders and other radical not-for-profits being stripped of their 501(c)(3) status.[28]

BLACK YOUTH PROJECT 100 (BYP100) AND THE BLACK QUEER FEMINIST LENS

While Black Lives Matter worked to create a national network and the Dream Defenders worked to build its base among poor and working-class people in the southeastern US, the city of Chicago also emerged as one the most important regional cites of struggle for the burgeoning movement against state violence. With the nurturance of activist scholars, University of Chicago political scientist Cathy Cohen and historian Barbara Ransby, the political organization BYP100 emerged as one of the most innovative new political forces in the aftermath of George Zimmerman's acquittal. Significantly, both Cohen and Ransby worked in the tradition of Civil Rights organizer Ella Baker by eschewing hierarchical masculine forms of charismatic leadership in favor of assisting young people to develop their own autonomous organizing modes.[29]

In contrast to the BLM network, which initially grew out of spontaneous social media activism, BYP100's roots lay in radical organizing circles at the University of Chicago and the University of Illinois. BYP, which stands for Black Youth Project, was founded by Cathy Cohen at University of Chicago in 2004. Cohen, who authored *The Boundaries of Blackness: AIDS and the Breakdown of Black Politics* and *Democracy Remixed: Black Youth and the Future of American Politics*, was not content to simply write about Black politics, but instead sought to channel university resources into grassroots activism.[30]

Eight years after Cohen's creation of the Black Youth Project, participants asked her to help provide the infrastructure for a national convening of Black youth activists. She successfully raised the money, and during the second week of July 2013, a hundred African American activists ages 18–35 met in Chicago for a week of political exchange, consciousness raising, and movement building. As one participant recalled, the desire to envision "Black Liberation beyond electoral politics" animated the gathering as young organizers—many of whom had undergraduate and postgraduate training—sought to expand the national political horizon "beyond the November moment" of Barack Obama's successful reelection campaign in 2012.[31]

Historical contingency influenced BYP100's founding. By happenstance, Florida authorities announced the acquittal of Zimmerman during BYP100's national convening in 2013, thereby profoundly shaping its trajectory. From 2004 through 2013, BYP nurtured an array of radical politics, including queer activism, labor rights, and feminism. However, this changed as the national outrage mounted over police killings of unarmed Black residents.

"Folks who attended that initial convening come from various parts of movements: there were artists, elected officials, folks who did LGBTQ rights organizing, gender justice organizers, folks from labor unions," remembered BYP100 cofounder Charlene Carruthers. "It was out of that moment that we decided to focus on mass criminalization and, really at the core of it, looking at anti-Blackness and its role in the oppression of Black folks, particularly in this country, but also worldwide."[32]

Privileging state violence and mass criminalization as its main target, the political goals of BYP100 hinged on three primary areas: electoral and civic participation, direct action, and public policy advocacy. Many participants saw the fight against law enforcement as part of a larger movement for Black Liberation. "The struggle against CPD [Chicago Police Department] is one aspect of the long-term struggle of abolishing anti-Blackness," argued Charlene Carruthers in February 2016. "Taking up the struggle for the sake of accountability in the killing of Black people like Laquan [McDonald] and Rekia [Boyd] is essential."[33] Since then the accomplishments of BYP100 have been remarkable. In 2015 their targeted activism forced Chicago state's attorney Anita Alvarez to resign, and for a moment, Mayor Rahm Emanuel's administration teetered as BYP100 led citywide protests against him.[34]

From its inception, BYP100 members identified an older generation of women activists, including Ella Baker, Audre Lorde, and Barbara Smith, as prime inspirations for how to blend a radical "queer feminist lens" with anti-capitalist politics. Closer to home, they relied on radical thinkers Cathy Cohen and Barbara Ransby as foundational to their vision of social transformation. "BYP100 is committed to training this generation and future generations of young Black activists to organize and mobilize in order to create transformative change for all Black people," explained Carruthers. "We do this work through what we call a 'Black queer feminist lens' because we believe that in order to achieve liberation for all Black folks we have to be radically inclusive—not just in our analysis, but also in our practice, in how we go about leadership. We believe that a Black Freedom Movement in our lifetime is possible."[35]

One of the most noteworthy dimensions of BYP100, BLM, and the larger Movement for Black Lives is that women are not only the majority of the activists, but they are also leading many of the national organizations. Of course, Black women's activism is not new. From Pauli Murray, Marian Wright Edelman, Coretta Scott King, Joanne Grant, Fannie Lou Hamer, and Ella Baker of the Civil Rights Movement, to Elaine Brown, Ericka Huggins, Kathleen Cleaver, and Angela Davis of the Black Panther and Communist Parties, African American women's activism has always been an integral part of the Black freedom struggle.[36] However, while the current Movement for Black Lives draws on these important foremothers, there are also some significant differences.

Perhaps the most striking feature of the contemporary BLMM/M4BL is the sheer numbers of women, nonbinary, and queer people in not only the rank-and-file, but also the leadership of organizations. From the cybernetic formation of BLM to the on-the-ground street protests in Sanford, Ferguson, and Baltimore, women composed an overwhelming majority. Their leadership has brought issues of gender, homophobia, and transphobia to the fore in ways that the social movements of the 1960s and 1970s failed to address. "To assert the significance of queer bodies as part of the Black community is new and important," argues Cathy Cohen.[37] "[Now] activists are saying that not only are gay, lesbian, trans, and queer folk part of our communities, but they are part of the leadership and they—for example, cis and trans women—have to be at the center of how we think about Black Liberation. The centering of cis and trans women and lesbians and gay men as members and leaders of our communities, that to me is significant and new."[38]

In order to understand why this has happened, it is necessary to reach back into the history of Black women's organizing over the past half century. While this story could easily begin with the mobilization of Black women's clubs in the formative years of Jim Crow segregation and the activism of early antilynching crusader Ida B. Wells, BLMM/M4BL's most immediate historical precedents stem from the modern Black freedom struggle, including the overlapping movements for Civil Rights, Black Power, Black Radicalism, and Black Feminism in the postwar era. For many contemporary activists, the Combahee River Collective and the concept of intersectionality were foundational influences.

"Our work is heavily influenced by [Kimberlé] Crenshaw's theory," explained Alicia Garza in a recent interview. "People think that we are engaged with identity politics. The truth is that we are doing what the labor movement has always done—organizing people at the bottom."[39] BLMM/M4BL's commitment to intersectionality and a queer feminist lens plays itself out in practical ways in BYP100's community organizing efforts. Janaé Bonsu explained,

> We aren't perfect, and we are in this constant effort to be who we say we are, when we say, we have a Black Feminist lens. Certainly, [we focus] on the most vulnerable, most marginalized, and we have a consensus driven democratic process in our decision-making. All those things are our core values, [but] sometimes . . . we mess up. And when that happens, you know on a chapter level or national level, I am appreciative of our ongoing commitment to right our wrongs.

To this end, BYP100 developed a strict policy of accountability for its membership and established a healing and safety council to reckon with conflict and injury inside the organization from larger social structures of heteropatriarchy, transphobia, and misogyny. BYP100 sees these problems not simply as externalities, but also as internal issues that remain integral to creating a viable movement for

Black Liberation. Bonsu saw these measures as essential to "help us heal ... and push through that, so we can continue to struggle."[40]

As the growth and development of these new organizations show, BLMM/M4BL has multiple layers and tendencies that reflect both the shared political culture of the national movement and the specificity of local communities. Just shy of the two-year anniversary of Michael Brown's shooting in Ferguson, Missouri, by police officer Darren Wilson, the Movement for Black Lives released a comprehensive statement of demands and policy prescriptions. "A Vision for Black Lives: Policy Demands for Black Power, Freedom, and Justice" provided a comprehensive blueprint for dismantling the carceral architecture of the last half century and reinvesting these resources in communities of color. Written at a moment of real optimism and possibility, as the ideas and sensibilities of BLMM/M4BL had thoroughly penetrated mainstream America, this document offered a concrete set of six core organizing demands with nearly thirty policy recommendations nested under each one. Invoking the structure of the historic Black Panther Party's Ten-Point Program, the document wed a tradition of grassroots radicalism to more conventional means of targeting municipal, state, and federal government through legislation, court challenges, and electoral mobilization.

A longtime activist with the Organization for Black Struggle, a grassroots protest group in St. Louis, Missouri, summed up the motivations behind this collective authorship of a set of concrete policy demands and organizing tools:

> Our grievances and solutions extend beyond the police killing of our people; state violence includes failing schools that criminalize our children, dwindling earning opportunities, wars on our trans and queer family that deny them of their humanity, and so much more. That's why we united, with a renewed energy and purpose, to put forth a shared vision of the world we want to live in.[41]

The longest and most detailed demand called for an "End to the

War on Black People," and its careful parsing of how to overturn the mechanisms of mass incarceration, state violence against African Americans and other populations of color, deportation, and the use of the state and federal death penalty reflected how the roots of the Black Lives Matter network were in the widespread protests against police killings of Black youth. Strikingly, successive demands for economic redistribution followed the insistence on ending institutionalized state violence. Redistributive concerns comprised half of the policy demands, including calls for reparations, economic justice, community control, and political power. "Invest/divest" represented one of the most compelling parts of the platform, thereby uniting the fights against material inequality and organized state violence.[42]

ASSATA TAUGHT ME AND THE REMIX
OF THE BLACK PANTHER PARTY'S LEGACY

Using the format of the Ten Point Program in the "Vision for Black Lives" platform underscored how historical memory of the BPP influenced BLMM/M4BL activists two generations removed from the upheaval of the 1960s. However, the ubiquity of New York BPP and BLA member Assata Shakur's words and image in BLMM/M4BL spaces represented the most immediate channeling of the Panthers' legacy. In the years after Trayvon Martin's killing, her name was emblazoned on T-shirts, immortalized by organizations such as Assata's Daughters, and invoked by M4BL protest chants. It mattered both that Assata Shakur was a woman and a dissident member of the BPP. Her iconography symbolized an alternate Black Feminist trajectory of struggle and resistance rooted in the experience of Black women's incarceration and fugitivity. A poem that Shakur wrote while in exile in Cuba during the 1980s became a movement anthem that opened and closed gatherings of BLM, BYP100, and many other groups involved in the Movement for Black Lives:

It is our duty to fight for our freedom.
It is our duty to win.
We must love each other and support each other.
We have nothing to lose but our chains.[43]

Contemporary activists' choice of Assata Shakur as political symbol reflects the needs of the present moment as well as a lesser-known
history of the Black Panther Party itself in which women sustained
the organization after 1968 by directing and staffing its longest running (and arguably most important) institutions—liberation schools,
breakfast programs, and other community survival efforts. Until quite
recently, many mainstream portrayals of the BPP focused almost exclusively on masculinist bravado and armed confrontation with the
state. Too often, sensational gunplay and the rhetoric of Panther leaders Huey Newton, Bobby Seale, and Eldridge Cleaver reduced the Party to a simplistic antagonist of a nonviolent Civil Rights Movement.
Indeed, the image of Bobby Seale holding a loaded shotgun standing
outside the California state house became one of the defining images
of the Black Power movement. Lost in this masculinist account is the
foundational role played by female leaders and rank-and-file members
of the BPP, ranging from Ericka Huggins and Cleo Silvers to Kathleen
Cleaver, Afeni Shakur, Brenda Byes, Connie Matthews, Sister Makin-
ya, Akua Njeri, Assata Shakur, and many, many others.

In addition to providing a gendered lens linking past and present, BLMM/M4BL's focus on Assata resonates not only because she
was a Panther, but also because she joined the organization's militant
successor, the Black Liberation Army, whose allies enabled her escape
to Cuba. In the 1980s and beyond, Shakur's writings served as an
important organizing tool that dramatized the scale of violence that
incarcerated women faced at all levels of the criminal justice system.
Moreover, her status as fugitive and exile showed that seemingly impossible victories could be won.[44] "Who else [is] better as a symbol

of resistance—from the New Jersey Turnpike, to being broken out of prison, to living in exile in Cuba," asked Ashley Yates, cofounder of Millennial Activists United in Ferguson, Missouri. "It's the real-life storyline of a Black woman legend." Yates designed the iconic T-shirt and hoodie, "Assata Taught Me," that became a standard-bearer in BLMM/M4BL protests. She later relocated to the Oakland area, in part to "soak up some of the organizing history" in the home of the Panthers. "I just hope people feel empowered by it and a sense of community when they wear it. I hope they feel the resistance, the ancestors, and unapologetically Black."[45]

Despite widespread identification with Assata Shakur and the iconography of the Black Panther Party, throughout its history, BLMM/M4BL has understood itself as a lateral network, rather than as a single organization or tendency. As a result, there are important differences from an older generation of Black radical groups from the 1960s that embraced state socialist principles. Although it is often forgotten in the three decades since the collapse of the Soviet Union and Eastern Bloc countries, the Panthers were, in fact, a Leninist "vanguard party" that practiced top-down democratic centralism. In this sense, the Party's contemporary image as the embodiment of Black Power is in tension with its internationalist history in which Black youth activists embraced Marxist revolutions in Cuba, Vietnam, and China, while defining themselves against the insular formulations of cultural nationalism. Given the disproportionate prosecution of Black left organizations by law enforcement in the 1960s and 1970s, much of this lived history has been denied future generations of activists. Deploying the tools of incarceration, infiltration, and state-sanctioned murder, one of the great successes of the Cold War's counterintelligence campaigns was to criminalize and silence popular expressions of Anti-imperialism and Third World and Black Marxism espoused by the Panthers, Revolutionary Action Movement, and other radical groups. "We're going to fight racism not with racism, but we're going to fight with solidarity," argued Fred Hampton shortly before he was killed by a joint operation of the Chicago Police Department and federal law enforcement. "We say we're not going to fight capitalism with black capitalism, but we're going to fight it with socialism."[46] Repression of the Black left, then and now, plays an important role in shaping the parameters of Black organizing.

In addition to insights about the effects of state violence, the Black Panther Party's trajectory offers some important lessons about the dangers of incorporation into a two-party, winner-take-all voting system that resists structural change. Like BLMM/M4BL's challenges today, the Panthers also faced the difficulty of integrating its local chapters throughout the United States with its national leadership, thereby creating rifts that left the whole organization vulnerable to state repression. As a New York Panther who witnessed the expulsion of the Panther 21 and many of the East Coast chapters, Assata Shakur herself fought for greater party democracy and sharing of resources with local activists on the ground. In 1972, when West Coast Panther leaders Bobby Seale and Elaine Brown ran for mayor and city council respectively, many regional chapters dissolved as the Central Committee diverted monies and personnel into the electoral campaigns in Oakland. This created deep resentment throughout the organization and furthered a damaging split out of which the Black Liberation Army emerged. As this example illustrates, the inherent tension between national leadership and the grassroots is not unique to BLMM/M4BL, nor are the dangers to social movements of being subsumed into the United States' two-party electoral system.[47]

CONCLUSION

While invoking the iconography of Assata Shakur, the Movement for Black Lives has created its own remix of Black Power ideas that speak to the urgent needs of the present. As Black female organizers have ascended to the forefront of the struggle against state violence and mass incarceration, they have drawn on registers of the Black Radical tradition that link antiracist and anti-capitalist critique to a queer, feminist lens. External struggles against state violence are inseparable from internal battles within family and community as gender, queer, and trans equity form the cornerstone of twenty-first century Black Liberation. Over the past eight years, BLMM/M4BL's politicization of "Black life" through mass protest against police killings has been crucial to expanding the movement for prison and police abolition that seeks to divest carceral institutions of state monies and to reinvest those resources into redistributive social services.

The BLMM/M4BL's imprint can be felt in many different aspects of American life, from the precedent-setting convictions of police officers for killings of unarmed Black people to a profound delegitimization of punishment as a way of life.[48] This seismic shift in common sense has influenced a broad spectrum of left organizing from the radical wing of the labor movement through municipal reform campaigns.[49] It is doubtful, for example, that progressive prosecutors and district attorneys like Larry Krasner, Chesa Boudin, and Rachael Rollins would have been elected without the massive uprisings and demonstrations that the Movement for Black Lives has nurtured over the past decade. While the electoral gains are important, the movement's greatest accomplishment exists outside the two-party system. After a half-century of rapidly escalating criminalization and incarceration, BLMM/M4BL has been the most sustained challenge to the bipartisan consensus around law and order campaigns and their racialized politics of state violence and mass incarceration.

One of the biggest issues currently facing the Movement for Black Lives is continuing to nurture the vibrancy of militant grassroots organizing efforts rooted in prison abolition, while its most visible icons engage the elite worlds of corporate media, philanthropy, and electoral politics. Given the far-right march of the United States during the

Trump Era, many progressive and radical groups have understandably forsworn their independence from the two-party system and engaged in voter registration and get-out-the-vote campaigns out of perceived necessity. And despite the blame placed on "defund the police" for down-ballot losses in the November 2020 elections by Representatives Abigail Spanberger, Jim Clyburn, and other centrist Democrats, there is ample evidence that voter participation increased in the areas with sustained BLMM/M4BL protests and radical organizing. In the presidential election of November 2020, large-scale turnout in cities with substantial Black populations such as Philadelphia, Milwaukee, and Detroit played a crucial role in Democrats taking back the three states that powered Donald Trump's 2016 electoral victory: Pennsylvania, Wisconsin, and Michigan. "I think that Black voters saw our votes as a form of protest," argued Alicia Garza in an interview with CNN. "Black voters saw a direct connection between protesting in the streets and protesting at the polls."[50] Similarly, in Georgia, the long-term coalition forged by Stacey Abrams in her 2018 gubernatorial run brought together Black Lives Matter, Mijente, Asian-American advocacy groups, and Southerners on New Ground.[51] Currently, there is greater "popular front" unity between social movement organizing and electoral politics than was seen under the Obama administration, during which large segments of BLMM/M4BL eschewed incorporation into the Democratic Party. One of the BLMM/M4BL's challenges will be to maintain its independence and to support its regional infrastructure throughout the country.

While the BLMM/M4BL successfully mobilized unprecedented numbers of Americans to participate in demonstrations for Black lives across the country, sustaining an organizing infrastructure that reaches down to the grassroots is an ongoing challenge. Conflict between local affiliates and national icons has been exacerbated by the Black Lives Matter Global Network Foundation's lack of financial transparency with the deluge of foundation and corporate monies it received; estimates are as high as 90 million dollars for 2020 alone.[52] These troubles are not unique; they have plagued a variety of organizations, from the top-down Black Panther Party with its central committee to lateral political formations such as Occupy Wall Street. Equally challenging, are the politics of celebrity in the era of social media, which further exacerbates the inevitable divide between national leadership and local activists. The Dream Defenders' decision to disconnect their social media feeds and focus on a community-based organizing model nurtured by lived experience and real-world relationships contains important lessons for us all. Finally, as Keeanga-Yamahtta Taylor has argued, one of the most important questions moving forward is how to engage and adapt the politics of solidarity to our current moment. Be it the War on Terror, the settler-colonial violence of the extractive industry, or the regime of mass deportation and criminalization of immigrants, it is clear that cross-racial and cross-class alignments are essential to fighting state violence at home and abroad. Here, once again, the words of Assata Shakur are an important resource for how to envision radical Black organizing while working in active coalition with others: "Any community seriously concerned with its own freedom has to be concerned about other peoples' freedom as well."[53]

ACKNOWLEDGMENTS

This volume is the product of overlapping networks of support, friendship, and solidarity. First and foremost, I would like to thank Anthony Arnove and Keeanga Yamahtta Taylor for their abiding interest, encouragement, and time in helping assemble these essays into a book. Haymarket staff Nisha Bosley, Rachel Cohen, Maya Marshall, Jim Plank, and Ashley Smith provided essential editorial, logistical, and public relations support as well. My writing partner, the brilliant historian Kim Butler has been an incredible companion and support through this journey. I am also deeply indebted to all of the people who were generous enough to speak with me and share invaluable knowledge and insight, including Ernest Allen, Janaé Bonsu, Charlene Carruthers, Patrisse Cullors, Emory Douglas, Rachael Gilmer, Beverly Jones, Talitha LeFlouria, members of Lost Voices, Beryl Satter, Nailah Summers, and many, many others. Cathy Cohen's and Barbara Ransby's Chicago convenings deeply informed this work, and I am grateful to them for their brilliance (and generosity) as scholars and organizers.

The vibrant political community of Nicole Burrowes, Robert Chase, Belinda Davis, Carlos Decena, Jaskiran Dhillon, Nicole Fleetwood, Nikol Alexander Floyd, Rebecca Givan, Kali Gross, Elizabeth Hinton, Malav Kanuga, Julilly Kohler-Hausmann, Kelly Lytle Hernandez, Khalil Muhammad, Rosemary Ndbuizu, Mary Louise Patterson, Susan Reverby, Jason Stanley, Heather Thompson, Lee Wengraf, Yohuru Williams, Sherry Wolf, Todd Wolfson, and Jason Wozniak have informed and nurtured so many different aspects of this book. I would also like to give a special thanks to Rutgers colleague and comrade Nancy Holstrom who pushed me to write "Ferguson's Inheritance" in 2014, which started an odyssey of publicly engaged writing that has been enormously satisfying. *Boston Review* has been crucial to this volume as a welcoming venue for intersectional, left scholarship and activism. Deborah Chasman, Liza Featherstone, Doug Henwood, Alex Lichtenstein, Adam McGee, Simon Waxman, and Komozi Woodard all provided crucial feedback and editorial support to particular essays in this collection. Ian Gavigan served as a thorough and insightful research assistant.

Harvard University's Charles Warren Center provided me with much needed time off and the incredible intellectual vibrancy of the Crime and Punishment Seminar, many thanks to Elizabeth Hinton, Walther Johnson, and Lisa McGirr for making this possible. Rutgers University's Department of History and the School of Arts and Sciences have also nurtured this book in innumerable ways, and I am very grateful for the resources that are so essential for research. Special thanks to the former Dean of the Humanities and current Founding Executive Director of the Institute for the Study of Global Racial Justice Michelle Stephens, who has provided generous support and a model of engaged leadership. My colleagues in African American and Diaspora history have been crucial for a life of the mind and of the heart, many thanks to those already named and to Carolyn Brown, Erica Dunbar, Tiffany Gill, and Deborah Gray White.

Finally, I owe everything I have done and who I am to the ancestors. I would like to express gratitude to my mother, my father, Carla Jean Tolson, Lucy Jean Murch, Michelle December Tindall, William Martin jr and sr, and the rest of the Martin family for their wisdom and unconditional love.

NOTES

This excerpt from "Affirmation" is reprinted from *Assata: An Autobiography* (Chicago: Lawrence Hill Books, 1987), 1.

INTRODUCTION

1. T. Hasan Johnson, "Inventing the Sister-Bandit Queen: Icon Construction and the Africana Imaginary in the Case of Assata Shakur" (PhD thesis, Claremont Graduate University, 2007), 10–11; Assata Shakur, *Assata: An Autobiography* (Westport, CT: Zed, 1987).
2. Teishan A. Latner, "Assata Shakur Is Welcome Here: Havana, Black Freedom Struggle and U.S. Cuba Relations," *Souls: A Critical Journal of Black Politics* 19, no. 4 (April 2018): 455–477.
3. Joseph Kaplan, "The Exile of Assata Shakur: Marronage and American Borderlands" (undergraduate thesis, University of Puget Sound, 2016), https://soundideas.pugetsound.edu/history_theses/19.
4. Elizabeth Hinton, *From the War on Poverty to the War on Crime: The Making of Mass Incarceration in America* (Cambridge, MA: Harvard University Press, 2016); Naomi Murakawa, *The First Civil Right: How Liberals Built Prison America* (Oxford: Oxford University Press, 2014).
5. Following the most comprehensive account of the Black Lives Matter movement to date, I have used Barbara Ransby's naming convention from *Making All Black Lives Matter: Reimagining Freedom in the 21st Century* (Berkeley: University of California Press, 2018). Throughout the book I refer to the larger Black Lives Matter movement/Movement for Black Lives as BLMM/M4BL.
6. Larry Buchanan, Quoctrung Bui, and Jugal K. Patel, "Black Lives Matter May Be the Largest Protest Movement in History," *New York Times*, July 3, 2020, https://www.nytimes.com/interactive/2020/07/03/us/george-floyd-protests-crowd-size.html; Rutgers American Association

of University Professors, American Federation of Teachers, and AFL-CIO, "Call to Action: Justice for George Floyd and Breonna Taylor," https://www.rutgersaaup.org/call-to-action-justice-for-george-floyd-and-breonna-taylor/.

7. Stuart Hall, *Policing the Crisis: Mugging, the State, and Law and Order,* 2nd ed. (New York: Palgrave Macmillan, 2013).

8. Keeanga-Yamahtta Taylor, "Five Years Later, Do Black Lives Matter?," *Jacobin,* September 30, 2019, https://jacobinmag.com/2019/09/Black-lives-matter-laquan-mcdonald-mike-brown-eric-garner; Keeanga-Yamahtta Taylor, *Black Lives Matter to Black Liberation* (Chicago: Haymarket Books, 2016).

9. Adrian Florido, "These Are the Minneapolis Activists Leading the Push To Abolish the Police," *NPR,* June 26, 2020, https://www.npr.org/2020/06/26/882001628/these-are-the-minneapolis-activists-leading-the-push-to-abolish-the-police; MPD150, "About MPD150" https://www.mpd150.com/about/.

10. Buchanan, Bui, and Patel, "Black Lives Matter May Be the Largest Protest Movement in History."

11. Robert A. Pape and Keven Ruby, "The Capitol Rioters Aren't Like Other Extremists," *Atlantic,* February 2, 2021, https://www.theatlantic.com/ideas/archive/2021/02/the-capitol-rioters-arent-like-other-extremists/617895/?fbclid=IwAR1BJJX_RpAFeghHyh3wSTugt-BZWGjAp1qw9Fe1eVgME351zcLZJAvUp-c.

12. Barbara Ransby, "The White Left Needs to Embrace Black Leadership," *Nation,* July 2, 2020, https://www.thenation.com/article/activism/black-lives-white-left/; Shakur, *Assata.*

CHAPTER 1

1. Huey P. Newton, *Revolutionary Suicide* (New York: Writers and Readers Publishing, Inc., 1973), 14.

2. Harry Haywood, *Negro Liberation* (Chicago: Liberator Press, 1976), 11.

3. Manning Marable, foreword to *The New Black Vote: Politics and Power in Four American Cities,* by Rod Bush (San Francisco: Synthesis Publications, 1984), 3; Nicholas Lemann, *The Promised Land: The Great Black Migration and How It Changed America* (New York: A.A. Knopf, 1991), 6.

4. Quoted by Albert S. Broussard, "In Search of the Promised Land:
    African American Migration to San Francisco, 1900–1945," in *Seeking
    El Dorado: African Americans in California*, Lawrence de Graaf et al.,
    eds. (Los Angeles: Autry Museum of Western Heritage, 2001), 190.

5. Charles Johnson, *The Negro War Worker in San Francisco* (San Francis-
    co: A Local Self-Survey, 1944), 1.

6. US Bureau of the Census, *Population by Age, Race, and Sex in Oakland,
    Calif. by Census Tracts: 1940.*

7. US Department of Labor, "Data from Census Bureau Estimates for
    Oakland, California," 1980 Census, Run No. 831120, 4.

8. For a sustained discussion of the complex relation of the Black Pan-
    ther Party to the concept of Black Power, see Donna Murch, "When
    the Panther Travels: Race and the Southern Diaspora in the History of
    the BPP, 1964–1972," Conference Paper, Diaspora and the Difference
    Race Makes Symposium, Black Atlantic Seminar, Rutgers University,
    February 16, 2007.

9. Donna Murch, "The Urban Promise of Black Power: African Ameri-
    can Political Mobilization in Oakland and the East Bay, 1961–1977"
    (PhD thesis, UC Berkeley, 2004).

10. After conducting extensive oral history interviews with activists
    in the Bay Area Black Power movement for my dissertation, I was
    struck by how many had served time in the California Youth Au-
    thority and other penal institutions. For a representative sample, see
    Emory Douglas, in conversation with author, March 7, 2002; Leon
    White, in conversation with author, August 9, 2002; Fritz Pointer,
    in conversation with author, March 12, 2002; Judith May, "Struggle
    for Authority: A Comparison of Four Social Change Programs in
    Oakland, California" (PhD thesis, UC Berkeley, 1973).

11. Newton, *Revolutionary Suicide*, 110–27; Ernest Allen, in conversation
    with author, February 3, 2002; Murch, "The Urban Promise of Black
    Power," 147; Paul Alkebulan, "The Role of Ideology in the Growth,
    Establishment, and Decline of the Black Panther Party: 1966 to 1982"
    (PhD thesis, UC Berkeley, 2003), 104.

12. Quote taken from Jeanne Theoharis, "'Alabama on the Avalon':
    Rethinking the Watts Uprising and the Character of Black Protest in
    Los Angeles," in *The Black Power Movement: Rethinking the Civil Rights–
    Black Power Era*, Peniel E. Joseph, ed. (New York: Routledge, 2006), 33.

13. Melvyn Newton, in conversation with author, March 15, 2002.

14. Albert Broussard, *Black San Francisco: The Struggle for Racial Equality in the West, 1900–1945* (Lawrence: University of Kansas, 1993); Gerald D. Nash, *The American West Transformed: The Impact of the Second World War* (Lincoln: University of Nebraska Press, 1985), 17.

15. Marilynn S. Johnson, *The Second Gold Rush: Oakland and the East Bay in World War II* (Berkeley and Los Angeles: University of California Press, 1993), 30.

16. Broussard, *Black San Francisco*, 192; Gretchen Lemke-Santangelo, *Abiding Courage: African American Women and the East Bay Community* (Chapel Hill: University of North Carolina Press, 1996); Johnson, *The Negro War Worker in San Francisco*.

17. According to Charles Johnson, in the 19–24 age group, women outnumbered men by 2 to 1; Johnson, *The Negro War Worker in San Francisco*, 6.

18. Lawrence B. de Graaf and Quintard Taylor, introduction to *Seeking El Dorado*, 24; Walter Bachemin, in conversation with author, June 28, 1998; William Henry Brown, "Class Aspects of Residential Development and Choice in Oakland Black Community" (PhD thesis, UC Berkeley, 1970), 86. This dynamic was reenacted inside the state itself. Large numbers of Southern migrants who first settled in Los Angeles, which had a much older and larger African American community, later chose to move north in search of a less hostile environment. Floyd Hunter, *Housing Discrimination in Oakland, California: A Study Prepared for the Oakland Mayor's Committee on Full Opportunity and the Council of Social Planning, Alameda County* (Berkeley, California, 1964), 14.

19. In my oral history interviews with migrants, this theme frequently emerged. See, for example, Melvyn Newton, 2002; Bachemin, 1998.

20. Donna Murch, "The Problem of the Occupational Color Line," unpublished paper, 15.

21. Charles Wollenberg, *Marinship at War: Shipbuilding and Social Change in Wartime Sausalito* (Berkeley, California: Western Heritage Press, 1990), 71.

22. C. L. Dellums, *International President of the Brotherhood of Sleeping Car Porters and Civil Rights Leaders*, Northern California Negro Political Series, Regional Oral History Office, Bancroft Library, UC Berkeley; Robert O. Self, *American Babylon: Race and the Struggle for Postwar*

· *Oakland* (Princeton: Princeton University Press, 2003).

23. Committee of Fair Employment Practice, "Final Report," June 28, 1946, Institute for Governmental Studies, University of California Berkeley, 77.

24. Oakland Police Department Report, 6, Oakland Public Library, 23; Johnson, *Second Gold Rush*; Murch, "The Problem of the Occupational Color Line."

25. Edward C. Hayes, *Power Structure and Urban Policy: Who Rules in Oakland?* (San Francisco: McGraw-Hill Book Company, 1972), 48.

26. Hayes, *Power Structure*, 44.

27. Hayes, *Power Structure*, 44; Johnson, *Second Gold Rush*, 167; Gretchen Lemke-Santangelo, "Deindustrialization, Urban Poverty and African American Community Mobilization in Oakland, 1945 through 1990s," in Graaf et al. eds., *Seeking El Dorado*, 343–76.

28. Johnson, *Second Gold Rush*, 167; Oakland Police Department Report, 6. This article was originally published in 2007 in *Souls, A Critical Journal of Black Politics, Culture and Society*; however, in her book, *From the War on Poverty to the War on Crime: The Making of Mass Incarceration in American* (Cambridge, MA: Harvard University Press, 2016), Elizabeth Hinton explores the importance of juvenile delinquency for punitive regimes at the federal level.

29. May, "Struggle for Authority," 115–17.

30. May, "Struggle for Authority," 115–17; Evelio Grillo, *Black Cuban, Black American: A Memoir* (Houston: Arte Publico Press, 2000), 131; Laura Mihailoff, "Protecting Our Children: A History of the California Youth Authority and Juvenile Justice, 1938–1968" (PhD diss., UC Berkeley, 2005).

31. May, "Struggle for Authority," 24.

32. May, "Struggle for Authority, 128.

33. May, "Struggle for Authority, 130; Oakland Police Department History 1941–1955, Part 6, 36–40, Oakland Oral History Room, Oakland Public Library.

34. May, "Struggle for Authority," 130–35; Oakland Police Department History 1941–1955, Part 6, 36–40.

35. May, "Struggle for Authority," 130.

36. Komozi Woodard, *A Nation within a Nation: Amiri Baraka (LeRoi Jones) & Black Power Politics* (Chapel Hill: University of North Caroli-

na Press, 1999); Self, *American Babylon*; Peniel E. Joseph, *Waiting 'Til the Midnight Hour: A Narrative History of Black Power in America* (New York: Henry Holt, 2006). For new literature on the history of Black Studies, see also Peniel E. Joseph, "Black Studies, Student Activism, and the Black Power Movement," in *The Black Power Movement*, 251–77 and Noliwe Rooks, *White Money, Black Power: The Surprising History of African American Studies and the Crisis of Race in Higher Education* (Boston: Beacon Press, 2006).

37. For a sustained discussion of the roots of the Bay Area Black Power movement in postwar struggles over California higher education, see Murch, "The Urban Promise of Black Power."

38. John Aubrey Douglass, "Brokering the 1960 Master Plan: Pat Brown and the Promise of California Higher Education," in *Responsible Liberalism: Edmund G. "Pat" Brown and Reform Government in California 1958–1967*, Martin Schiesl, ed. (Los Angeles: Edmund G. "Pat" Brown Institute of Public Affairs, 2003), 86; John Aubrey Douglass, *The California Idea and American Education: 1850 to the 1960 Master Plan* (Stanford: Stanford University Press, 2007); Sidney W. Brossman and Myron Roberts, *California Community Colleges* (Palo Alto, CA: Field Educational Publications, 1973).

39. "Completion Levels: Percentage of High School and College 'Completers' (Aged 25 and Over) in Selected Cities, 1969,'" *Historical Statistics of Black America*, Jessie Carney Smith and Carrell Peterson Horton, eds. (Detroit: Gale Research, 1995), 530.

40. Jonathan Spencer, "Caught in Crossfire: Marcus Foster and America's Urban Education Crisis, 1941–1973" (PhD thesis, New York University, 2002), 361–63.

41. Jonathan Spencer quotes an article from 1952 in which the planners of the new McClymonds building described how their choice of design suited "the modified curriculum" meant to "fit the needs of the pupils in the area." Although biology was still required, McClymonds possessed a different "set of contents and set of objectives . . . [with] a good deal of attention . . . to the care of the hair, skin and feet." Spencer, "Crossfire," 361.

42. Spencer, "Crossfire," 363.

43. Warden, "Letters to the Ice Box," *Daily California*, March 1, 1961; March 22, 1961.

44. Murch, "The Urban Promise," 99.
45. Lisa Rubens, "Interview with Donald Hopkins," unpublished transcript, Regional Oral History Office, UC Berkeley, September 29, 2000.
46. Ernest Allen, in conversation with author, July 3, 2001.
47. Maurice Dawson, in conversation with author, July 26, 2002; Khalid Al Mansour, in conversation with author, July 22, 2002.
48. Dawson, 2002; Al Mansour, 2002.
49. Scot Brown, *Fighting for US: Maulana Karenga, the US Organization, and Black Cultural Nationalism* (New York: New York University Press, 2003), 25–29.
50. Dawson, 2002.
51. Al Mansour, 2002; Khalid Al Mansour, *Black Americans at the Crossroads–Where Do We Go from Here?* (New York: First African Arabian Press, 1990).
52. Brown, *Fighting for US*, 28.
53. James Edward Smethurst, *The Black Arts Movement: Literary Nationalism in the 1960s and 1970s* (Chapel Hill: University of North Carolina Press, 2005), 260–62.
54. Dawson, 2002; Timothy Tyson, "Introduction: Robert F. Williams, 'Black Power,' and the Roots of the African American Freedom Struggle," in Robert F. Williams, *Negroes with Guns* (Detroit: Wayne State University Press, 1998), xxvii.
55. Dawson, 2002.
56. Al Mansour, 2002.
57. Newton, *Revolutionary Suicide*, 60–66; Bobby Seale, *Seize the Time* (New York: Random House, 1970), 21; Mary Lewis, in conversation with author," March 18, 2002.
58. Allen, 2001.
59. Melvyn Newton, 2002.
60. Gabrielle Morris, *Head of the Class: An Oral History of African American Achievement in Higher Education and Beyond* (New York: Twayne Publishers, 1995), xvii–xviii.
61. "Special Report on Minority Group Relations Presented to the Trustees," *Peralta Colleges Bulletin* 5, no. 8 (January 12, 1968): 2.
62. Eric Hobsbawm, *Primitive Rebels: Studies in Archaic Forms of Social Movement in the 19th and 20th Centuries* (New York: W. W. Norton & Company, 1959), 108.

63. Seale, *Seize the Time*, 3–6.
64. Seale, *Seize the Time*, 3–12.
65. Newton, *Revolutionary Suicide*, 69.
66. Seale, *Seize the Time*, 26, 30.
67. Leo Bazile, in conversation with author, February 19, 2001.
68. Seale, *Seize the Time*, 20.
69. Seale, *Seize the Time*, 30–31.
70. Newton, *Revolutionary Suicide*, 108–9.
71. David Hilliard and Lewis Cole, *This Side of Glory: The Autobiography of David Hilliard and the Story of the Black Panther Party* (New York: Little, Brown, 1993), 228; Robyn Ceanne Spencer, "Repression Breeds Resistance: The Rise and Fall of the Black Panther Party in Oakland, California, 1966–1982" (PhD thesis, Columbia University, 2001), 44.
72. Newton, *Revolutionary Suicide*, 115–16.
73. Melvyn Newton, 2002.
74. Interestingly, Warden distanced himself from the successes at Merritt rather than claiming credit. He described the Merritt student movement with the following, "That leadership tended to be what the press would call more militant, more radical, and out of that grew the Black Panther movement." Newton, *Revolutionary Suicide*, 72; Al Mansour, 2002.

CHAPTER 2

1. Jeremi Suri, *Power and Protest: Global Revolution and the Rise of Detente* (Cambridge, MA: Harvard University Press, 2003).
2. Donna Murch, *Living for the City: Migration, Education, and the Rise of the Black Panther Party in Oakland, California* (Chapel Hill: University of North Carolina Press, 2010), 72.
3. Amy Wallace and Dave Lesher, "UC Regents, in Historic Vote, Wipe Out Affirmative Action," *Los Angeles Times*, July 21, 1995, http://articles.latimes.com/1995-07-21/news/mn-26379_1_regents-vote-affirmative-action-university-of-california-regents.
4. Robin D. G. Kelley, *Yo' Mama's Disfunktional! Fighting the Culture Wars in Urban America* (Boston: Beacon Press, 1997); Todd Gitlin,

The Sixties: Years of Hope, Days of Rage (New York, 1987); Gitlin, *The Twilight of Common Dreams: Why America Is Wracked by the Culture Wars* (New York, 1996).

5. David Horowitz, *Hating Whitey and Other Progressive Causes* (Dallas: Spence Publishing Company, 1999). This vibrant body of scholarship is too expansive to list here comprehensively; for an overview, see Peniel E. Joseph, "The Black Power Movement: A State of the Field," *Journal of American History* 96, no. 3 (2009): 751–76; Jacquelyn Dowd Hall, "The Long Civil Rights Movement and the Political Uses of the Past," *Journal of American History* 91, no. 4 (2005): 1233–63; Hasan Kwame Jeffries, *Bloody Lowndes: Civil Rights and Black Power in Alabama's Black Belt* (New York: New York University Press, 2010); Rhonda Y. Williams, *Concrete Demands: The Search for Black Power in the 20th Century* (New York: Taylor and Francis, 2014).

6. Elizabeth Hinton, *From the War on Poverty to the War on Crime: The Making of Mass Incarceration in America* (Cambridge, MA: Harvard University Press, 2016); Heather Ann Thompson, "Why Mass Incarceration Matters: Rethinking Crisis, Decline, and Transformation in Postwar American History," *Journal of American History* 97, no. 3 (2010): 703–34; Thompson, "State-Building, Carcerality, and the Fate of Racial Justice and Economic Equality in Postwar America," paper presented at the Crime and Punishment in American History Workshop, Charles Warren Center for Studies in American History, Harvard University, Cambridge, Massachusetts, March 27, 2018; Murch, *Living for the City*, 184.

7. Hinton, *From the War on Poverty to the War on Crime*, 2–4, 30–52, 245, 294; Thompson, "Why Mass Incarceration Matters."

8. Ashley D. Farmer, *Remaking Black Power: How Black Women Transformed an Era* (Chapel Hill: University of North Carolina Press, 2017), 2, 159–68; Frances M. Beal, *Double Jeopardy: To Be Black and Female* (pamphlet, New York, 1969); Kimberlé Crenshaw, "Demarginalizing the Intersection of Race and Sex: A Black Feminist Critique of Antidiscrimination Doctrine, Feminist Theory and Antiracist Politics," *University of Chicago Legal Forum*, no. 1 (1989): 139–67. See also Crenshaw, "Mapping the Margins: Intersectionality, Identity Politics, and Violence against Women of Color," *Stanford Law Review* 43, no. 6 (1991): 1241–99; Dan Berger, *Captive Nation: Black Prison Organizing in the Civil Rights Era* (Chapel Hill: University of North Carolina Press, 2014).

CHAPTER 3

1. Kelefa Sanneh, "Body Count," *New Yorker*, September 14, 2015, http://www.newyorker.com/magazine/2015/09/14/body-count-a-critic-at-large-kelefa-sanneh.

2. Michael Fortner, *Black Silent Majority: The Rockefeller Drug Laws and the Politics of Punishment* (Cambridge, MA: Harvard University Press, 2015); Michelle Alexander, *The New Jim Crow: Mass Incarceration in the Age of Colorblindness* (New York: The New Press, 2010).

3. Alexander, *The New Jim Crow*, 11, 56.

4. Fortner, *Black Silent Majority*,13.

5. Fortner, *Black Silent Majority*, 23.

6. Fortner, *Black Silent Majority*, ix.

7. Fortner, *Black Silent Majority*, 63, 153.

8. Donna Murch, *Living for the City: Migration, Education, and the Rise of the Black Panther Party in Oakland, California* (Chapel Hill: University of North Carolina Press, 2010); Julilly Kohler-Hausmann, "'The Attila the Hun Law': New York's Rockefeller Drug Laws and the Making of a Punitive State," *Journal of Social History* 44 (Fall 2010): 71–96.

9. Fortner, *Black Silent Majority*, 16.

10. Fortner, *Black Silent Majority*, 9.

11. Fortner, *Black Silent Majority*, 206–7.

12. Fortner, *Black Silent Majority*, 64.

13. Khalil Gibran Muhammad, "'Black Silent Majority,' by Michael Javen Fortner," *New York Times*, September 21, 2015, https://www.nytimes.com/2015/09/27/books/review/Black-silent-majority-by-michael-javen-fortner.html. See exchange in Facebook group Historians Confront the Carceral State: https://www.facebook.com/groups/historiansconfrontthecarceralstate/permalink/878848982183177.

14. Fortner, *Black Silent Majority*, 256.

15. Michael Javen Fortner, "The Real Roots of '70s Drug Laws," *New York Times*, September 28, 2015, https://www.nytimes.com/2015/09/28/opinion/the-real-roots-of-70s-drug-laws.html.

16. Gabor Maté, *In the Realm of Hungry Ghosts: Close Encounters with Addiction* (Berkeley, CA: North Atlantic Books, 2010).

CHAPTER 4

1. John Nielsen, "Police Using Battering Ram Seize Cocaine, 1 Suspect," *Los Angeles Times*, March 23, 1985; Patricia Klein and Stephanie Chavez, "Pacoima Leaders Protest Police Use of Motorized Battering Ram," *Los Angeles Times*, February 9, 1985; Daryl F. Gates, *Chief: My Life in the LAPD* (New York: Bantam Books, 1992), 279.

2. Stuart Hall et al., *Policing the Crisis: Mugging, the State, and Law and Order* (New York: Palgrave Macmillan, 2013); Clarence Lusane, *Pipe Dream Blues: Racism and the War on Drugs* (Boston: South End Press, 1991).

3. Anti-Drug Abuse Act of 1986, H.R. 5484, 99th Cong. (1986); William D. Montalbano, "Latins Push Belated War on Cocaine," *Los Angeles Times*, December 1, 1985, A1.

4. Heather Ann Thompson, "Why Mass Incarceration Matters: Rethinking Crisis, Decline, and Transformation in Postwar America," *Journal of American History*, 97 (December 2010): 703–35; Marc Mauer, *Race to Incarcerate: The Sentencing Project* (New York: The New Press, 1999), 33; Michelle Alexander, *The New Jim Crow: Mass Incarceration in the Age of Colorblindness* (New York: The New Press, 2010), 59; Dan Baum, *Smoke and Mirrors: The War on Drugs and the Politics of Failure* (New York: Back Bay Books, 1996), 259.

5. On antidrug campaigns in the postwar era, see Baum, *Smoke and Mirrors*; Kathleen J. Frydl, *The Drug Wars in America, 1940–1973* (New York: Cambridge University Press, 2013); and Julilly Kohler-Hausmann, "Forging a Punishing State: The Punitive Turn in US Criminal and Social Policy, 1968–1980" (PhD diss., University of Illinois, 2010). On the declaration of war, see Susan Sontag, "Real Battles and Empty Metaphors," *New York Times*, September 10, 2002, http://www.nytimes.com/2002/09/10/opinion/real-battles-and-empty-metaphors.html; Jerome H. Skolnick, "A Critical Look at the National Drug Control Strategy," *Yale Law and Policy Review* 78, no. 1 (1990): 75–116.

6. On gang databases, see Max Felker-Kantor, "Managing Marginalization from Watts to Rodney King: The Struggle over Policing and Social Control in Los Angeles, 1965–1992" (PhD diss., University of Southern California, 2014), 381–83. For statistics on nearly half of African American men in Los Angeles County under age twenty-five as gang members,

see Nina Siegel, "Ganging Up on Civil Liberties," *Progressive* 61 (Oct. 1997): 28–31; Ruth Wilson Gilmore, *Golden Gulag: Prisons, Surplus, Crisis, and Opposition in Globalizing California* (Berkeley and Los Angeles: University of California Press, 2007), 108. For the statistic of 25 percent of detainees in the Los Angeles County Jail for drug possession in 1990, see Joe Domanick, *To Protect and to Serve: The LAPD's Century of War in the City of Dreams* (Los Angeles: Figueroa Press, 2003), 322. On Los Angeles as site of world's largest urban prison population, see John C. Quicker, Yvonne Nunley Galeai, and Akil Batani-Khalfani, *Bootstrap or Noose: Drugs in South Central Los Angeles* (unpublished manuscript in author's possession); and Edward W. Soja, *Postmodern Geographies: The Reassertion of Space in Critical Social Theory* (London and New York: Verso Books, 1989), 193. On the extreme racial disparities of mass incarceration and the War on Drugs, see Michael Tonry, *Malign Neglect: Race, Crime, and Punishment in America* (Oxford and New York: Oxford University Press, 1995); Marc Mauer and Ryan S. King, "A 25-Year Quagmire: The 'War on Drugs' and Its Impact on American Society," The Sentencing Project (Washington, DC, 2007). On the statistic that African Americans were roughly 7 percent of California's population but 31 percent of the state's prisoners, see Gilmore, *Golden Gulag*, 108, 110–11, 185; "California 2000. Census 2000 Profile," August 2002, US Census Bureau, http://www.census.gov/prod/2002pubs/c2kprof00-ca. pdf; Thompson, "Why Mass Incarceration Matters"; Alexander, *The New Jim Crow*; and Baum, *Smoke and Mirrors*.

7. Domanick, *To Protect and to Serve*, 11–12, 207–8. On the origins of the Los Angeles Special Weapons and Tactics Team (SWAT) and its use against the Southern California Black Panther Party and the Symbionese Liberation Army, see Gates, *Chief*, 105–23, 131–39, 355. For official institutional histories of SWAT within the Los Angeles Police Department (LAPD), see "S.W.A.T.," LAPD: Official Site of the Los Angeles Police Department, http://www.lapdonline.org/inside_the_lapd/content_basic_view/848; "History of S.W.A.T.," ibid., http://www.lapdonline.org/metropolitan_division/content_basic_ view/849; and "History of the Metro Division," ibid., http://www. lapdonline.org/metropolitan_division/content_basic_view/6359.

8. Felker-Kantor, "Managing Marginalization from Watts to Rodney King," 141, 368, 372, 377; Gates, *Chief*, 292.

9. On the LAPD Air Support Division as the world's largest law enforcement system, see Domanick, *To Protect and to Serve*, 112; Eric Malnic, "Sky Patrol Arm of the Law Goes to New Heights through Helicopter Units in LAPD's Air Support Division," *Los Angeles Times*, April 3, 1988, http://articles.latimes.com/1988-04-03/local/me-972_1_air-support-division; and "History of the Air Support Division," LAPD: Official Site of the Los Angeles Police Department, http://www.lapdonline.org/air_support_division/content_basic_view/1179. Felker-Kantor, "Managing Marginalization from Watts to Rodney King," 421.

10. Gates, *Chief*, 287; Ronald J. Ostrow, "Casual Drug Users Should Be Shot, Gates Says," *Los Angeles Times*, September 6, 1990, A19. For Daryl F. Gates's argument for greater incarceration rates, see Felker-Kantor, "Managing Marginalization from Watts to Rodney King," 409–10.

11. On racialization and gang arrest, see Domanick, *To Protect and to Serve*, 328–29. For the lieutenant's thoughts on organized crime, see Quicker, Galeai, and Batani-Khalfani, *Bootstrap or Noose*, 30; Francisco Delgado, "The Drugs Connection: Cocaine Is Big Business on Southland's Shady Sidewalks," *Long Beach Press Telegram*, December 16, 1986; and Felker-Kantor, "Managing Marginalization from Watts to Rodney King," 369, 409, 412. On the move toward seeing gangs and drug trafficking as organized crime and terrorism, see ibid., 378; Domanick, *To Protect and to Serve*; Baum, *Smoke and Mirrors*, 141–42; Racketeer Influenced and Corrupt Organizations (RICO) Act, 84 Stat. 941 (1970); Mike Davis, "Los Angeles: Civil Liberties between the Hammer and the Rock," *New Left Review* 1 (July–August 1988): 44; Beth Caldwell, "Criminalizing Day-to-Day Life: A Socio-Legal Critique of Gang Injunctions," *American Journal of Criminal Law* 37 (Summer 2010): 245; and Siegel, "Ganging Up on Civil Liberties."

12. On the Gang Reporting Evaluation and Tracking system (GREAT) and other gang databases, see Felker-Kantor, "Managing Marginalization from Watts to Rodney King," 381–83. On the overrepresentation of Black youth in GREAT, see ibid., 404–5; Davis, "Los Angeles"; and Siegel, "Ganging Up on Civil Liberties." On gang injunctions and on the inability to hire lawyers, see Caldwell, "Criminalizing Day-to-Day Life," 241–90.

13. California Street Terrorism Enforcement and Prevention Act of 1988, Cal. Pen. Code 186.20. On the California Street Terrorism Enforcement

and Prevention Act and its revisions in 2007 and 2013, see Gilmore, *Golden Gulag*, 108; Sara Lynn Hofwegen, "Unjust and Ineffective: A Critical Look at California's STEP Act," *Southern California Interdisciplinary Law Journal* 18 (Spring 2009): 679–701; Alex Alonso, telephone conversation with author, May 8, 2014 (unarchived); "California Criminal Street Gang Offenses and Enhancements," n.d., First District Appellate Project, http://wiki.fdap.org/main_page/gangs; and "Juvenile Crime. Initiative Statute: Text of Proposition 21," Vote 2000, http://primary2000.sos.ca.gov/VoterGuide/Propositions/21text.htm.

14. Baum, *Smoke and Mirrors*, 250. On the mass arrests of April 9, 1988, see Gates, *Chief*, 293; Davis, "Los Angeles," 37; and Felker-Kantor, "Managing Marginalization from Watts to Rodney King," 400–403. On the costs of "Operation Hammer," see Robert Welkos, "700 Seized in Gang Sweeps," *Los Angeles Times*, September 19, 1988, B21; and Quicker, Galeai, and Batani-Khalfani, *Bootstrap or Noose*, 16.

15. For an exception to the lack of work on responses by communities of color to changing punishment regimes, see Max Felker-Kantor, "Managing Marginalization from Watts to Rodney King." For competing views on how African American and Latino populations experienced the war(s) on drugs, see Vesla M. Weaver, "Frontlash: Race and the Development of Punitive Crime Policy," *Studies in American Political Development* 21 (Fall 2007), 230–65; Michael Javen Fortner, "The Carceral State and the Crucible of Black Politics: An Urban History of the Rockefeller Drug Laws," ibid., 27 (April 2013), 14–35; and Maxine Waters, "Drugs, Democrats and Priorities," *Nation*, July 24, 1989, 141.

16. João H. Costa Vargas, *Catching Hell in the City of Angels: Life and Meanings of Blackness in South Central Los Angeles* (Minneapolis: University of Minnesota Press, 2006), 119–21.

17. For a theorization of the concepts of crisis and moral panic, see Hall, *Policing the Crisis*.

18. Felker-Kantor, "Managing Marginalization from Watts to Rodney King," 357–58, 365, 389–96; Darnell Hunt and Ana-Christina Ramon, eds., *Black Los Angeles: American Dreams and Racial Realities* (New York: New York University Press, 2010); Edward J. Boyer, "Dual Goal Told at Rally: Strike at Crime, Win Olympic Funds," *Los Angeles Times*, July 15, 1985, B1.

19. Felker-Kantor, "Managing Marginalization from Watts to Rodney

King," 397, 388. For a contrasting take on intraracial class divisions during New York's drug war under Gov. Nelson A. Rockefeller, see Fortner, "Carceral State and the Crucible of Black Politics."

20. Karen Bass, "Alcohol's Relationship to Urban Violence: When Free Enterprise Threatens Community Welfare," in *Black-Korean Encounter: Toward Understanding and Alliance*, ed. Eui-Young Yu (Los Angeles: Regina Books, 1994), 5, 6, 70–72; Angela Hill, "California Lawmaker Works to Improve Her Community," *Crisis* 112 (March–April 2005), 8. On the use of forfeiture-seizure money to finance drug treatment, see Karen Bass, "Application for Crack Cocaine Conference," Fall 1989, folder 6, box 35, Liberty Hill Foundation Records (Southern California Library, Los Angeles). On the mission of the Community Coalition for Substance Abuse Prevention and Treatment, see Bass, "Alcohol's Relationship to Urban Violence," 6; Kyeyoung Park, "The Morality of a Commodity: A Case of 'Rebuilding L.A. without Liquor Stores,'" *Amerasia Journal* 21 (Winter 1995–96): 1–24; and Bass, "Application for Crack Cocaine Conference."

21. On the motto of the Coalition Against Police Abuse, see Mary Pauline Roche, "Unfinished Business: The Production of Resistance to State Violence in London and Derry" (PhD diss., University of Southern California, 2004), 154; and Vargas, *Catching Hell in the City of Angels*, 109–40. On the increases in numbers of African Americans and Latinos in the California Department of Corrections, see Gilmore, *Golden Gulag*, 111, table 4.

22. Vargas, *Catching Hell in the City of Angels*, 109–40, 177–213; Fortner, "Carceral State and the Crucible of Black Politics": Julilly Kohler-Hausmann, "'The Attila the Hun Law': New York's Rockefeller Drug Laws and the Making of a Punitive State," *Journal of Social History* 44 (Fall 2010): 71–96.

23. On the rates of African American incarceration in 1995, see Gilmore, *Golden Gulag*, 110–11; and "California 2000."

CHAPTER 5

1. Michelle Alexander, *The New Jim Crow: Mass Incarceration in the Age of Colorblindness* (New York: The New Press, 2010); Naomi Murakawa,

The First Civil Right: How Liberals Built Prison America (New York: Oxford University Press, 2014); Christian Parenti, *Lockdown America: Police and Prisons in the Age of Crisis* (New York: Verso, 1999).

2. "Full Video of Hillary Clinton's Meeting with Black Lives Matters Activists," *Democracy Now!*, August 19, 2015.

3. See chapter 3, my review of recent scholarship about the Rockefeller era for context: "Who's to Blame for Mass Incarceration?," originally published in *Boston Review*, October 16, 2015.

4. "Full Video of Hillary Clinton's Meeting."

5. Lee Fang, "Private Prison Lobbyists Are Raising Cash for Hillary Clinton," *Intercept*, July 23, 2015.

6. Alexander, *The New Jim Crow*, 9.

7. While incarceration rates are much worse for Black men, rates for Black women in the United States are also high: as of 2001, lifetime rates were 1 in 19 for Black women compared to 1 in 181 for white women. The Sentencing Project, "Incarcerated Women Fact Sheet" (revised September 2012).

8. Alexander, *The New Jim Crow*.

9. Jon F. Hale, "The Making of the New Democrats," *Political Science Quarterly* 110, no. 2 (1995): 215.

10. Hale, "New Democrats," 212.

11. Hale, "New Democrats," 218–25; Thomas Ferguson and Joel Rogers, *Right Turn: The Decline of the Democrats and the Future of American Politics* (New York: Hill and Wang, 1986).

12. Robert C. Smith, *We Have No Leaders: African Americans in the Post-Civil Rights Era* (Albany: State University of New York Press, 1996), 256.

13. This whole section is heavily indebted to the pathbreaking research of eminent political scientist Robert C. Smith; see Smith, *We Have No Leaders*, 255–57. I was not able to obtain a copy of the report, but I am including its full citation for those interested in further research. Milton Kotler and Nelson Rosenbaum, "Strengthening the Democratic Party through Strategic Marketing: Voters and Donors," a confidential report for the Democratic National Committee by the CRG Research Institute, Washington, DC, 1985. Stanley Greenberg, *Report on Democratic Defection*, Washington, DC, 1985, as quoted in Thomas Edsall and Mary Edsall, *Chain Reaction: The Impact of Race, Rights*

and Taxes on American Politics (New York: W. W. Norton, 1992), 182. The Edsalls published an article succinctly titled "Race" in the *Atlantic Monthly* in 1991 that parroted similar claims.

14. Smith, *We Have No Leaders*, 255.
15. Ferguson and Rogers, *Right Turn*, 207–32; Lance Selfa, *The Democrats: A Critical History* (Chicago: Haymarket, 2008), 63–85; Ian Haney López, *Dog Whistle Politics: How Coded Racial Appeals Have Reinvented Racism and Wrecked the Middle Class* (New York: Oxford University Press, 2014).
16. Hale, "New Democrats," 225.
17. "Willie Horton 1988 Attack Ad," available on YouTube, https://www. youtube.com/watch?v=Io9KMSSEZ0Y.
18. Jonathan Simon, *Governing through Crime: How the War on Crime Transformed American Democracy and Created a Culture of Fear* (New York: Oxford University Press, 2007), 57.
19. Hale, "New Democrats," 221–25.
20. Hale, 226–27. For collusion of the Congressional Black Caucus in the Reagan-era drug war, see Donna Murch, "Crack in Los Angeles: Crisis, Militarization, and African American Response to the Late Twentieth-Century War on Drugs," *Journal of American History* 102, no. 1 (Summer 2015): 162–73.
21. Marshall Frady, "Death in Arkansas," *New Yorker*, February 22, 1993, 107, 126–32; Simon, *Governing through Crime*, 69.
22. Simon, *Governing through Crime*, 66–70; Frady, "Death in Arkansas," 132.
23. Paul D'Amato, "The Democrats and the Death Penalty," *International Socialist Review* 6 (Spring 1999).
24. Selfa, *The Democrats*, 79.
25. This quotation is taken from a summary by Murakawa, *The First Civil Right*, 143.
26. Alexander, *The New Jim Crow*, 55.
27. Gerald Horne, "Black Fire: 'Riot' and 'Revolt' in Los Angeles, 1965 and 1992," Lawrence B. DeGraaf, Kevin Mulroy, and Quintard Taylor, eds., *Seeking El Dorado: African Americans in California* (Seattle: University of Washington Press, 2015), 377–404; Murakawa, *The First Civil Right*, 142; Parenti, *Lockdown America*, 63–66.
28. Fang, "Private Prison Lobbyists Are Raising Cash"; Helen Redmond,

"Are the Drug Warriors Ready to Surrender?," *Socialist Worker*, August 26, 2015.

29. Dan Merica, "Bill Clinton Says He Made Mass Incarceration Issue Worse," CNN, July 15, 2015, https://www.cnn.com/2015/07/15/politics/bill-clinton-1994-crime-bill/index.html.

30. Alexander, *The New Jim Crow*, 55.

31. Alexander, *The New Jim Crow*, 58–94; D'Amato, "The Democrats and the Death Penalty."

32. Selfa, *The Democrats*, 79.

33. Murakawa, *The First Civil Right*, 141–46.

34. Selfa, *The Democrats*, 84.

35. Robert Parry, "Ronald Reagan: Worst President Ever?," *Common Dreams*, June 3, 2009.

36. Charles P. Pierce, "Bill Clinton Apologizes for His Role in America's Prison Epidemic," *Esquire*, July 16, 2015.

37. Several scholars have explored how the incarcerated, convicted felons, and illicit drug users and sellers have come to signify the antithesis of citizenship. See, for example, Julilly Kohler-Hausmann, "'The Attila the Hun Law': New York's Rockefeller Drug Laws and the Making of a Punitive State," *Journal of Social History* 44 (Fall 2010): 71–95.

38. Patrick Healy and Katharine Q. Seelye, "Clinton Says She 'Misspoke' about Dodging Sniper Fire," *New York Times*, March 25, 2008; Robert Parry, "Hillary Clinton's Failed Libya 'Doctrine,'" Consortiumnews.com, October 22, 2015.

CHAPTER 6

1. "The Murder of Emmett Till," *The American Experience*, Civil Rights Collection, January 20, 2003, https://www.pbs.org/wgbh/american-experience/films/till/.

2. Robert Stephens II, "In Defense of the Ferguson Riots," *Jacobin*, August 14, 2014, https://www.jacobinmag.com/2014/08/in-defense-of-the-ferguson-riots/.

3. Frances Robles and Julie Bosman, "Autopsy Shows Michael Brown Was Struck at Least Six Times," *New York Times*, August 17, 2014, http://www.nytimes.com/2014/08/18/us/michael-brown-autopsy-

shows-he-was-shot-at-least-6-times.html?_r=0.

4. Shawn Gude, "Why Baltimore Rebelled," *Jacobin*, April 28, 2015, https://www.jacobinmag.com/2015/04/baltimore-freddie-gray-unrest-protests/.

5. Mychal Denzel Smith, "A Q&A with Alicia Garza, Cofounder of #BlackLivesMatter," *Nation*, March 24, 2015, https://www.thenation.com/article/qa-alicia-garza-cofounder-Blacklivesmatter/.

6. "Ferguson October: Thousands March in St. Louis for Police Reform and Arrest of Officer Darren Wilson," *Democracy Now!*, October 13, 2014, http://www.democracynow.org/2014/10/13/thousands_march_in_ferguson_for_police; "Freedom Summer Mississippi," 1964, https://www.pbs.org/wgbh/americanexperience/films/freedomsummer/.

7. "Demonstrators 'Disrupt' St. Louis Symphony Singing a 'Requiem for Mike Brown,'" YouTube, October 5, 2014, https://www.youtube.com/watch?v=T_7ErkQFduQ.

8. "Demonstrators 'Disrupt' St. Louis Symphony."

9. Ari Berman, "North Carolina's Moral Mondays," *Nation*, July 17, 2013, https://www.thenation.com/article/north-carolinas-moral-mondays. I participated in one of these protests and observed this shaming of the police first hand.

10. "James Baldwin's National Press Club Speech (1986)," YouTube video, 53:37, December 22, 2014, https://www.youtube.com/watch?v=7_1ZEYgtijk.

11. "Watts Riots," Events, Civil Rights Digital Library, last modified February 23, 2018, http://crdl.usg.edu/events/watts_riots/?Welcome.

12. Alex Elkins, "The Origins of Stop-and-Frisk," *Jacobin*, May 9, 2015, https://www.jacobinmag.com/2015/05/stop-and-frisk-dragnet-ferguson-baltimore/.

13. Michael Gould-Wartofsky, "When Rioting Is Rational," *Jacobin*, January 2, 2015, https://www.jacobinmag.com/2015/01/when-rioting-is-rational-ferguson/; Douglas S. Massey and Nancy A. Denton, *American Apartheid: Segregation and the Making of the Underclass* (Cambridge, MA: Harvard University Press, 1993); Gerald Horne, "Black Fire: 'Riot' and 'Revolt' in Los Angeles, 1965 and 1992," in *Seeking El Dorado: African Americans in California*, Lawrence B. de Graaf, Kevin Mulroy, and Quintard Taylor, eds. (Seattle: University of Washington Press, 2001), 377–404; Bayard Rustin, "'Black Power and Coalition Politics,'

Commentary, September 1966, https://www.commentarymagazine.
com/articles/bayard-rustin-2/black-power-and-coalition-politics.

14. Donna Murch, *Living for the City: Migration, Education, and the Rise of
the Black Panther Party in Oakland, California* (Chapel Hill: University
of North Carolina Press, 2010), 66; Murch, "The Many Meanings of
Watts: Black Power, Wattstax, and the Carceral State," *OAH Magazine
of History* 26, no. 1 (January 2012): 37–40, https://doi.org/10.1093/
oahmag/oar062; Keeanga-Yamahtta Taylor, *From #BlackLivesMatter to
Black Liberation* (Chicago: Haymarket Books, 2016).

15. Christian Parenti, "The Making of the American Police State," *Jacobin*,
July 28, 2015, https://www.jacobinmag.com/2015/07/incarcera-
tion-capitalism-Black-lives-matter/.

16. Parenti, "The Making of the American Police State."

17. Heather Thompson's *Whose Detroit? Politics, Labor, and Race in An
American City* (Ithaca, NY: Cornell University Press, 2001); Murch,
Living for the City; Yohuru Williams, *Black Politics/White Power: Civil
Rights, Black Power, and the Black Panthers in New Haven* (Hoboken,
New Jersey: Wiley-Blackwell Publishing, 2000).

18. US Department of Justice, "Investigation of the Ferguson Police Department," March 2015, https://www.justice.gov/sites/default/files/
opa/press-releases/attachments/2015/03/04/ferguson_police_de-
partment_report.pdf.

19. Sarah Stillman, "Taken," *New Yorker*, August 12, 2013, http://www.
newyorker.com/magazine/2013/08/12/taken.

20. Malcolm X, "Message to the Grassroots," November 10, 1963, https://
www.blackpast.org/african-american-history/speeches-african-ameri-
can-history/1963-malcolm-x-message-grassroots/, accessed June 14, 2021.

CHAPTER 7

1. "Strange Bedfellows: Why Are the Koch Brothers & Van Jones
Teaming Up to End Mass Incarceration?," *Democracy Now!*, July 15,
2015, http://www.democracynow.org/201 5/7/15/strange_bedfel-
lows_why_are_the_koch.

2. Robert D. Putnam, "Unhappy Days for America," review of *Our
Kids: The American Dream in Crisis* by Nicholas Lemann, *New York*

Review of Books, May 21, 2015, http://www.nybooks.com/articles/2015/05/21/our-kids-unhappy-days-america/.

3. Louis Hyman, in conversation with author, April 29, 2016.

4. See, for example, Alex Lichtenstein, *Twice the Work of Free Labor: The Political Economy of Convict Labor in the New South* (New York: Verso, 1996); Talitha LeFlouria, *Chained in Silence: Black Women and Convict Labor in the New South* (Chapel Hill: University of North Carolina, 2016).

5. W. E. B. Du Bois, *The Souls of Black Folk* (New York: Penguin Books, 1989), 104.

6. Garland Brinkley, "One Dies, Get Another: Convict Leasing in the American South, 1866–1928," Economic History Association: EH Net, https://eh.net/book_reviews/one-dies-get-another-convict-leasing-in-the-american-south-1866-1928, accessed June 14, 2021; Matthew Mancini, *One Dies, Get Another: Convict Leasing in the American South, 1866–1928* (Columbia: University of South Carolina Press, 1996).

7. Douglas Blackmon, *Slavery by Another Name: The Re-Enslavement of Black Americans from the Civil War to World War II* (New York: Doubleday, 2008).

8. Talitha LeFlouria, in conversation with the author, June 11, 2016.

9. Paul Kiel and Annie Waldman, "The Color of Debt: How Collection Suits Squeeze Black Neighborhoods," ProPublica, October 5, 2015, https://www.propublica.org/article/debt-collection-lawsuits-squeeze-Black-neighborhoods.

10. Kiel and Waldman, "The Color of Debt."

11. Beryl Satter, in conversation with the author, May 3, 2016; Kiel and Waldman, "The Color of Debt"; Rakesh Kochhar and Anthony Cilluffo, "How Wealth Inequality Has Changed in the U.S. since the Great Recession, by Race, Ethnicity, and Income," Pew Research Center, November 1, 2017 (accesssed June 14, 2021), https://www.pewresearch.org/fact-tank/2017/11/01/how-wealth-inequality-has-changed-in-the-u-s-since-the-great-recession-by-race-ethnicity-and-income.

12. Noah Feldman, "Missing Student Loan Payments Shouldn't End in Handcuffs," *Chicago Tribune*, February 19, 2016, http://www.chicagotribune.com/news/opinion/commentary/ct-student-loan-payments-20160219-story.html.

13. Eli Hager, "Debtors' Prisons, Then and Now: FAQ," The Marshall Project, February 24, 2015.

14. Hager, "Debtors' Prisons."

15. Alicia Bannon, Mitali Nagrecha, and Rebekah Diller, "Criminal Justice Debt: A Barrier to Reentry," Brennan Center for Justice, 2010, https://www.brennancenter.org/our-work/research-reports/criminal-justice-debt-barrier-reentry, 4.

16. Mike Maciag, "Skyrocketing Court Fines Are Major Revenue Generator for Ferguson," *Governing*, August 22, 2014, http://www.governing.com/topics/public-justice-safety/gov-ferguson-missouri-court-fines-budget.html.

17. Walter Johnson, "Ferguson's Fortune 500 Company," *Atlantic*, April 26, 2015, http://www.theatlantic.com/politics/archive/2015/04/fergusons-fortune-500-company/390492/.

18. Maciag, "Skyrocketing Court Fines Are Major Revenue Generator for Ferguson."

19. Bannon, Nagrecha, and Diller, "Criminal Justice Debt."

20. Hager, "Debtors' Prisons, Then and Now: FAQ," 3.

21. Eric Markowitz, "Chain Gang 2.0: If You Can't Afford this GPS Ankle Bracelet, You Get Thrown in Jail," *International Business Times*, September 21, 2015, http://www.ibtimes.com/chain-gang-20-if-you-cant-afford-gps-ankle-bracelet-you-get-thrown-jail-2065283.

22. Markowitz, "Chain Gang."

23. Markowitz, "Chain Gang."

24. Bannon, Nagrecha, and Diller, "Criminal Justice Debt," 1.

25. Hager, "Debtors' Prisons, Then and Now: FAQ."

26. Bannon, Nagrecha, and Diller, "Criminal Justice Debt," 20, 22; Allyson Fredericksen and Linnea Lassite, "Debtors' Prison Redux: How Legal Loopholes Let Courts Across the Country Criminalize Poverty," Alliance for a Just Society, December 2015, https://www.prisonlegalnews.org/media/publications/Debtors%20Prisons%20Redux%20-%20How%20Legal%20Loopholes%20Let%20Courts%20Criminalize%20Poverty%2C%20AJS%2C%202015.pdf.

27. Bannon, Nagrecha, and Diller, "Criminal Justice Debt," 6, 29.

28. Bannon, Nagrecha, and Diller, "Criminal Justice Debt," 3–4, 29.

29. US Department of Justice, "Investigation of the Ferguson Police Department," March 2015, https://www.justice.gov/sites/default/files/

opa/press-releases/attachments/2015/03/04/ferguson_police_department_report.pdf.

30. Matt Apuzzo, "Justice Dept. Condemns Profit-Minded Court Policies Targeting the Poor," *New York Times*, March 14, 2016, http://www.nytimes.com/2016/03/15/us/politics/justice-dept-condemns-profit-minded-court-policies-targeting-the-poor.html.

31. Catherine Thorbecke, "Colorado Springs Will Repay Those Sent to Debtor's Prison in Landmark Settlement," ABC News, May 5, 2016, http://abcnews.go.com/US/colorado-springs-pay-debtors-prison-landmark-settlement/story?id=38905750.

32. Jack Denton, "Prison Labor Strike in Alabama: 'We Will No Longer Contribute to Our Own Oppression,'" *CounterPunch*, May 6, 2016, https://www.counterpunch.org/2016/05/06/prison-labor-strike-in-alabama-we-will-no-longer-contribute-to-our-own-oppression/; "Alabama Prison Strike Organizer Speaks from Behind Bars: We Are Engaged in a Struggle for Our Lives," *Democracy Now!*, May 13, 2016, http://www.democracynow.org/2016/5/13/alabama_prison_strike_organizer_speaks_from.

CHAPTER 8

1. Dan Merica, "Trump Pushes Death Penalty for Some Drug Dealers," CNN, March 19, 2019, https://www.cnn.com/2018/03/19/politics/opioid-policy-trump-new-hampshire/index.html.

2. Rajan Menon, "Forget the Wall—the Opioid Crisis Is Trump's Real National Emergency," *Nation*, January 31, 2019, https://www.thenation.com/article/archive/forget-the-wall-the-opioid-crisis-is-trumps-real-national-emergency/; CDC, "Understanding the Epidemic," https://www.cdc.gov/drugoverdose/epidemic/index.html; CDC, "Prescription Opioid Data," https://www.cdc.gov/drugoverdose/data/prescribing.html.

3. Menon, "Forget the Wall," *Nation*, January 31, 2019; Nabarun Dasgupta, Leo Beletsky, and Daniel Ciccarone, "Opioid Crisis: No Easy Fix to Its Social and Economic Determinants," *American Journal of Public Health* 108, no. 2 (February 2018): 2; American Society of Addition Medicine, "Opioid Addition 2016 Facts and Figures,"

https://www.asam.org/docs/default-source/advocacy/opioid-addiction-disease-facts-figures.pdf.

4. Julie Netherland and Helena Hansen, "White Opioids: Pharmaceutical Drugs and the War on Drugs That Wasn't," *Biosocieties* 12, no. 2 (June 2017): 217–38, https://www.ncbi.nlm.nih.gov/pmc/articles/PMC5501419/.

5. Jerry Kuzmarov, "The US War on Drugs: From its Origins to the Age of Trump," Historians for Peace and Democracy, March 14, 2018, https://www.historiansforpeace.org/wp-content/uploads/2018/02/Kuzmarov-War-on-Drugs.pdf.

6. Attorney General Jeff Sessions, "Remarks to the International Association of Chiefs of Police," US Department of Justice, October 23, 2017, https://www.justice.gov/opa/speech/attorney-general-sessions-delivers-remarks-international-association-chiefs-police?utm_medium=email&utm_source=govdelivery.

7. Edwin Meese III, "Jeff Sessions Is the Most Underrated Member of the Trump Administration," *USA Today*, January 30, 2018, https://www.usatoday.com/story/opinion/2018/01/30/jeff-sessions-most-underrated-member-trump-administration-edwin-meese-column/1074410001/.

8. Netherland and Hansen, "White Opioids."

9. Drug Policy Alliance, "A Brief History of the War on Drugs," https://drugpolicy.org/issues/brief-history-drug-war.

10. Keith Wailoo, *Pain: A Political History* (Baltimore: Johns Hopkins University Press, 2015), 170–75.

11. Art Van Zee, "The Promotion and Marketing of OxyContin: Commercial Triumph, Public Health Tragedy," *American Journal of Public Health* 99, no. 2 (February 2009): 222.

12. Van Zee, "Promotion and Marketing of OxyContin," 222.

13. Van Zee, "Promotion and Marketing of OxyContin," 222.

14. Van Zee, "Promotion and Marketing of OxyContin," 222.

15. Hansen and Netherland, "White Opioids," 15.

16. Hansen and Netherland, "White Opioids," 15.

17. David Herzberg, *Happy Pills in America: From Miltown to Prozac* (Baltimore: John Hopkins University Press, 2009); David Herzberg, in conversation with the author, December 29, 2018.

18. Drug Policy Alliance, "Race and the Drug War," http://www.drugpol-

icy.org/issues/race-and-drug-war.

19. David Herzberg, "Entitled to Addiction? Pharmaceuticals, Race and America's First Drug War," *Bulletin of the History of Medicine* 91, no. 3 (2017): 586–623.

20. Herzberg, "Entitled to Addiction," 587.

21. Herzberg, "Entitled to Addiction," 616.

22. Herzberg, "Entitled to Addiction," 590.

23. Dan Weikel, "The War on Crack Targets Minorities over Whites," *LA Times*, May 21, 1995, http://articles.latimes.com/1995-05-21/news/mn-4468_1_crack-cocaine.

24. Robert Pear, "Senate Confirms Trump Nominee Alex Azar as Health Secretary," *New York Times*, January 24, 2018, https://www.nytimes.com/2018/01/24/us/politics/alex-azar-health-and-human-services-secretary-confirmed-senate.html; Robert Reich, "Why Won't Trump Take on Big Pharma?," *Newsweek*, May 18, 2018, https://www.newsweek.com/robert-reich-why-wont-trump-takebig-pharma-opinion-931240.

25. Harry G. Levine and Drug Policy Alliance, "New York City's Marijuana Arrest Crusade . . . Continues," September 2009, https://drugpolicy.org/sites/default/files/Levine_NYC_MJ_Arrest_Crusade_Continues_Sept_2009.pdf.

26. Allen St. Pierre, "Marijuana Arrest: Devastation of a Life Well Lived," *Norml*, December 26, 2013; Paul Armentano, "New York City: Still the Marijuana Arrest Capital of the World," *Norml*, February 2, 2012. Both articles available at https://blog.norml.org/tag/giuliani/.

27. Michael Massing, "Winning the Drug War Isn't So Hard After All," *New York Times Magazine*, September 6, 1998, https://www.nytimes.com/1998/09/06/magazine/winning-the-drug-war-isn-t-so-hard-after-all.html.

28. Barry Meier, *Pain Killer: An Empire of Deceit and the Origin of America's Opioid Epidemic Pain Killer* (New York: Random House, 2003), 145–46.

29. Chris McGreal, "Rudy Giuliani Won Deal for OxyContin Maker to Continue Sales of Drug behind Opioid Deaths," *Guardian*, May 22, 2018, https://www.theguardian.com/us-news/2018/may/22/rudy-giuliani-opioid-epidemic-oxycontin-purdue-pharma.

30. Meier, *Pain Killer*, 145–46.

31. McGreal, "Rudy Giuliani Won."
32. Meier, *Pain Killer*; Beth Macy, *Dopesick: Dealers, Doctors, and the Drug Company That Addicted America* (New York: Little, Brown, 2018); Chris McGreal, *American Overdose: The Opioid Tragedy in Three Acts* (New York: PublicAffairs, 2018); Sam Quinones, *Dreamland: The True Tale of America's Opiate Epidemic* (Bloomsbury, 2015).
33. See *Democracy Now!* interview with Barry Meier, June 1, 2018, https://www.democracynow.org/2018/6/1/pain_killer_author_ barry_meier_on.
34. Children's Rights, "Children in the Cross Hairs: The Opioid Epidemic and Foster Care," June 19, 2018, https://www.childrensrights.org/ children-in-the-cross-hairs-the-opioid-epidemic-and-foster-care/; Jennifer Egan, "Children of the Opioid Crisis," *New York Times*, May 9, 2018, https://www.nytimes.com/2018/05/09/magazine/children-of-the-opioid-epidemic.html.
35. Testimony of Keith Humphreys to House Judiciary, Subcommittee on Immigration and Border Security, Hearing on the Immigration and the Opioid Crisis, February 15, 2018, https://republicans-judiciary.house.gov/wp-content/uploads/2018/02/Witness-Testimony-Keith-Humphreys.pdf.

CHAPTER 9

1.   Evan Hill, Ainara Tiefenthäler, Christiaan Triebert, Drew Jordan, Haley Willis, and Robin Stein, "How George Floyd Was Killed in Police Custody," *New York Times*, May 31, 2020, updated November 5, 2020, , https://www.nytimes.com/2020/05/31/us/george-floyd-investigation. html; Elizabeth Hinton, "The Minneapolis Uprising in Context," *Boston Review*, May 29, 2020, http://bostonreview.net/race/elizabeth-hinton-minneapolis-uprising-context; Mark Berman, John Sullivan, Julie Tate, and Jennifer Jenkins, "Protests Spread over Police Shootings. Police Promised Reforms. Every Year, They Still Shoot and Kill Nearly 1,000 People," *Washington Post*, June 8, 2020, https://www.washingtonpost.com/investigations/protests-spread-over-police-shootings-police-promised-reforms-every-year-they-still-shoot-nearly-1000-people/2020/06/08/5c204f0c-a67c-11ea-b473-04905b1af82b_story.html.

2.   Rukmini Callimachi, "Breonna Taylor's Life Was Changing. Then the Police Came to Her Door," *New York Times*, August 30, 2020, https://www.nytimes.com/2020/08/30/us/breonna-taylor-police-killing.html; Bridget Read, "What We Know about the Killing of Breonna Taylor," *Cut*, September, 29, 2020, https://www.thecut.com/2020/09/breonna-taylor-louisville-shooting-police-what-we-know.html.

3.   Minnesota Department of Health, "People in Poverty in Minnesota," https://data.web.health.state.mn.us/poverty_basic#race.

4.   Ta-Nehisi Coates, "Fear of a Black President," *Atlantic*, September 2012, https://www.theatlantic.com/magazine/archive/2012/09/fear-of-a-black-president/309064/; Young Turks, "Picture of Trayvon Martin Lying Dead Released (Graphic Image Warning)," YouTube, accessed January 8, 2017, https://www.youtube.com/watch?v=-Jiby_-of0RU; Alexander Cockburn, "You Really Think the Killer of Trayvon Martin Will Ever Do Time?," 28–29, in *Killing Trayvons: An Anthology of American Violence*, Kevin Alexander Gray, JoAnn Wypijewski, and Jeffrey St. Clair, eds. (Petrolia, CA: CounterPunch, 2014).

5.   Amanda Robb, "Meet George Zimmerman's Family," *GQ*, September 24, 2014, http://www.gq.com/story/george-zimmerman-family-values.

6.   "Trayvon Martin: Guilty of Being Black," *Nation*, editorial, April 16, 2012; Adam M. Butz, Michael P. Fix, and Joshua L. Mitchell, "Policy Learning and the Diffusion of Stand-Your-Ground Laws," *Politics & Policy* 43, no. 3 (June 2015): 347–77.

7.   Cockburn, "You Really Think the Killer of Trayvon Martin Will Ever Do Time?" (emphasis added).

8.   Butz, Fix, and Mitchell, "Policy Learning and the Diffusion of Stand-Your-Ground Laws"; Nicole Flatow and Rebecca Leber, "5 Disturbing Facts about the State of Stand Your Ground on the Second Anniversary of Trayvon's Death," *ThinkProgress*, February 26, 2014, https://thinkprogress.org/5-disturbing-facts-about-the-state-of-stand-your-ground-on-the-second-anniversary-of-trayvons-death-7ccf54e3a1d8; Beth Richie, *Arrested Justice: Black Women, Violence and America's Prison Nation* (New York: New York University Press, 2012).

9.   Paul Ortiz, *Emancipation Betrayed: The Hidden History of Black Organizing and White Violence in Florida from Reconstruction to the Bloody Election of 1920*, 1st ed. (Berkeley and Los Angeles: University of California Press, 2006).

10. Jeff Guo, "What People Don't Get about 'Black Twitter,'" *Washington Post*, October 22, 2015, https://www.washingtonpost.com/news/wonk/wp/2015/10/22/why-it-can-be-offensive-to-use-the-term-Black-twitter/.

11. Bernice J. Reagon, "A Borning Struggle," *New Directions* 7, no.3 (1980), https://dh.howard.edu/cgi/viewcontent.cgi?article=1236&-context=newdirections. Civil rights leader Bernice Johnson Reagon uses the phrase "borning" to describe catalytic developments that deeply influence political culture and inspire multiple movements for social justice: "The Civil Rights Movement was a borning struggle, breaking new ground and laying the foundation for ever-widening segments of the society to call for fundamental rights and human dignity. Few forces have created as many ripples that crossed racial, class, and social lines as did the Civil Rights Movement." BLMM/M4BL has been such a moment, and it has multiple trajectories, including prison abolition and renewed anti-capitalist/anti-austerity struggle. See, for example, Donna Murch, "The Amazon Union Drive Showed Us the Future of US Labor," *Guardian*, April 27, 2021, https://www.theguardian.com/commentisfree/2021/apr/27/amazon-union-drive-us-labor-future.

12. Gray, St. Clair, and Wypijewski, *Killing Trayvons*.

13. Wesley Lowery, "Black Lives Matter: Birth of a Movement," *Guardian*, January 17, 2017, https://www.theguardian.com/us-news/2017/jan/17/black-lives-matter-birth-of-a-movement; Jelani Cobb; "Where Is Black Lives Matter Headed?," *New Yorker*, March 14, 2016, https://www.newyorker.com/magazine/2016/03/14/where-is-black-lives-matter-headed.

14. Jewish Women's Archive, "Alicia Garza," https://jwa.org/people/garza-alicia; Yael Chanoff and Chanelle Ignant, "Garza Making Black Lives Matter with Pride," *Bay Area Reporter*, June 25, 2015, http://www.ebar.com/pride/article.php?sec=pride&article=175.

15. Alicia Garza, "A Herstory of the #Black Lives Matter Movement," *Feminist Wire*, October 7, 2014, http://www.thefeministwire.com/2014/10/Blacklivesmatter-2/.

16. Lowery, "Birth of a Movement."

17. Garza, "A Herstory."

18. Nicholas Fandos, "Protestors Confront Candidates on Race at a

Netroots Nation Conference," *New York Times,* July 8, 2015, https://
www.nytimes.com/2015/07/19/us/protesters-confront-candi-
dates-on-race-at-netroots-nation-conference.html; Barbara Ransby,
Making All Black Lives Matter: Reimagining Freedom in the 21st Century
(Berkeley: University of California Press, 2018), 75–77.

19. Garza, "A Herstory."
20. Garza, "A Herstory." For a contrary view, see Sofia Arias, "Solidarity Is
    Not Co-Optation," *Socialist Worker,* March 5, 2015, and Keeanga-Ya-
    mahtta Taylor, *From #BlackLivesMatter to Black Liberation* (Chicago:
    Haymarket Books, 2016), 186–190.
21. Nailah Summers, in conversation with the author, August 9, 2017;
    Abby Goodnough, "8 Acquitted in Death of Boy, 14, in Flori-
    da," *New York Times,* October 13, 2007, https://www.nytimes.
    com/2007/10/13/us/13bootcamp.html; Joan Mar, "Meet the Dream
    Defenders: 5 Key Members—What Have the DDs Achieved?,"
    Daily Kos, September 20, 2013, https://www.dailykos.com/
    story/2013/9/20/1239998/-Meet-the-Dream-Defenders-5-Key-
    Members-What-Have-the-DDs-Achieved; Rich Phillips, "Feds: No
    Civil Right Charges in Teen's Florida Boot Camp Death," CNN, April
    17, 2010, http://www.cnn.com/2010/CRIME/04/16/florida.boot.
    camp.death/index.html; Jim Avila, "Boot Camp Death—Caught on
    Tape," ABC News, April 28, 2007, http://abcnews.go.com/2020/
    story?id=2751785&page=1; Barbara Liston, "Dream Defenders, A
    New Generation, Fights for Civil Rights in Florida (PHOTOS),"
    Huffington Post, October 24, 2013, http://www.huffingtonpost.
    com/2013/08/24/dream-defenders-florida_n_3805651.html;
    Lizette Alvarez, "Florida Sit-In against 'Stand Your Ground,'" *New York
    Times,* August 11, 2013, https://www.nytimes.com/2013/08/12/us/
    dream-defenders-arent-walking-out-on-their-florida-protest.html.
22. Phillip Agnew, "Dream Defender Phillip Agnew Inspired by Martin
    Lee Anderson," YouTube, July 25, 2013, accessed October 11, 2017,
    https://www.youtube.com/watch?v=dVvosdfIpV8; Nailah Summers,
    in conversation with the author, August 9, 2017; Dream Defenders,
    "Team," http://www.dreamdefenders.org/team.
23. "Team," Dream Defenders; Summers, 2017; Rachael Gilmer, in con-
    versation with the author, August 16, 2017; Ransby, *Making All Black
    Lives Matter,* 34–36.

24. Summers, 2017; Gilmer, 2017.

25. Gilmer, 2017.

26. "About," Dream Defenders, http://www.dreamdefenders.org/about.

27. Gilmer, 2017; Dream Defenders, "Social Media Blackout," September 21, 2015, http://www.dreamdefenders.org/smBlackout; Dream Defenders, "Our Social Media Blackout Is Over," December 1, 2015, http://www. dreamdefenders.org/smBlackoutstatement; Dream Defenders, "Blackout Reflection: The Opium of the People," December 9, 2015, http://www. dreamdefenders.org/socialmedia_opium; Mychal Denzel Smith, "How Trayvon Martin's Death Launched a New Generation of Black Activism," *Nation*, August 27, 2014 https://www.thenation.com/article/how-tray-von-martins-death-launched-new-generation-of-Black-activism.

28. Gilmer, 2017.

29. For the most comprehensive account to date on the BYP100, see Ransby, *Making All Black Lives Matter*.

30. Cathy J. Cohen, *The Boundaries of Blackness: AIDS and the Breakdown of Black Politics* (Chicago: University of Chicago Press, 1999); Cathy J. Cohen, *Democracy Remixed: Black Youth and the Future of American Politics* (New York and Oxford: Oxford University Press, 2012); Smith, "New Generation of Black Activism."

31. Salim Muwakkil, "Not Your Grandfather's Black Freedom Movement: An Interview with BYP100's Charlene Carruthers," *In These Times*, February 8, 2016, http://inthesetimes.com/article/18755/char-lene-carruthers-on-byp200-Laquan-McDonald-and-police-violence; Sarah Jackson, "Ask a Feminist: Cathy Cohen on Black Lives Matter, Feminism," *Windy City Times*, December 12, 2015, http://www. windycitymediagroup.com/lgbt/Ask-a-Feminist-Cathy-Cohen-on-Black-Lives-Matter-feminism/53822.html.

32. Muwakkil, "Not Your Grandfather's Black Freedom Movement"; Charlene Carruthers, in conversation with the author, November 12, 2016; Janaé Bonsu, in conversation with the author, November 23, 2016.

33. Bonsu, 2016.

34. Black Youth Project 100, "Official Statement from the BYP100 on the Firing of CPD Police Superintendent Garry McCarthy," December 1, 2015, http://byp100.org/official-statement-from-the-byp100-on-the-firing-of-cpd-police-superintendent-garry-mccarthy/.

35. Muwakkil, "Not Your Grandfather's Black Freedom Movement."
36. Jackson, "Ask a Feminist."
37. Jackson, "Ask a Feminist."
38. Jackson, "Ask a Feminist."
39. Cobb, "Where Is Black Lives Matter Headed?," 10–11.
40. Bonsu, 2016.
41. Trymaine Lee, "Black Lives Matter Releases Policy Agenda," NBC News, August 1, 2016, http://www.nbcnews.com/news/us-news/Black-lives-matter-releases-policy-agenda-n620966.
42. Lee, "Black Lives Matter Releases Policy Agenda"; The Movement for Black Lives, "Platform," https://policy.m4bl.org/platform/, accessed November 13, 2017.
43. Garza, "A Herstory"; Assata Shakur, "To My People," *The Talking Drum*, July 4, 1973, http://www.thetalkingdrum.com/tmp.html.
44. Assata Shakur, *Assata: An Autobiography* (Chicago: Lawrence Hill Books, 2001).
45. Lamont Lilly, "Ferguson Activist Ashley Yates Talks Oakland, Assata Shakur, and Black Woman Leadership," *Truthout*, July 15, 2017, https://truthout.org/articles/ferguson-activist-ashley-yates-talks-oakland-assata-shakur-and-Black-woman-leadership.
46. "Fred Hampton - Political Prisoner," posted on Youtube January 6, 2013, https://www.youtube.com/watch?v=Wy1gveC3GVs.
47. Shakur, *Assata*, 223–234; Donna Murch, *Living for the City: Migration, Education, and the Rise of the Black Panther Party in Oakland, California* (Chapel Hill: University of North Carolina Press, 2010); Maya King, "Black Lives Matter Power Grab Sets Off Internal Revolt," *Politico*, December 10, 2020. https://www.politico.com/news/2020/12/10/black-lives-matter-organization-biden-444097.
48. Mariame Kaba, *We Do This 'Til We Free Us: Abolitionist Organizing and Transforming Justice* (Chicago: Haymarket Books, 2021).
49. See Murch, "Amazon Showed Us the Future."
50. Brandon Tensley, "How Black Voters and Simmering Protests Contributed to Trump's Loss," CNN, November 10, 2020, https://www.cnn.com/2020/11/10/politics/alicia-garza-Black-lives-matter-election-joe-biden/index.html.
51. Tensley, "Simmering."
52. Keeanga-Yamahtta Taylor, "Five Years Later, Do Black Lives Matter?";

Associated Press, "BLM's Patrisse Cullors to Step Down from Movement Foundation," *Politico*, May 27, 2021, https://www.politico.com/news/2021/05/27/black-lives-matter-patrisse-cullors-491275.

53. Taylor, *From #BlackLivesMatter to Black Liberation*; Rhonda Williams, *Concrete Demands: The Search for Black Power in the Twentieth Century* (New York: Routledge, 2013), 228.

INDEX

ABOUT THE AUTHOR

DONNA MURCH is an associate professor of history at Rutgers, the State University of New Jersey, and is the New Brunswick Chapter President of the Rutgers AAUP-AFT. She is the author of *Living for the City: Migration, Education, and the Rise of the Black Panther Party in Oakland, California* (University of North Carolina Press).